Desert Rats
at War

Desert Rats at War

2 ~ Europe

George Forty

LONDON
IAN ALLAN LTD

First published 1977

ISBN 0 7110 0733O

Design by Anthony Wirkus LSIAD

© George Forty, 1977

Published by Ian Allan Ltd, Shepperton, Surrey,
and printed in the United Kingdom by
Ian Allan Printing Ltd.

Contents

1939 **1945**

FROM
EL ALAMEIN
TO
BERLIN
VIA
AFRICA
TALY
FRANCE
BELGIUM
HOLLAND
GERMANY

7ᵀᴴ ARMOURED DIVISION

When the 7th Armoured Division entered Berlin in the summer of 1945, they erected a stone monument at the end of the Autobahn and Avus. The monument, which is a record of the Division's route from El Alamein to Berlin, consists of a rectangular stone plaque showing Divisional signs, place names and dates. Road works being carried out by the Germans in the area of the monument made it necessary for it to be taken down and moved to England where the Staff College has provided a lasting and final site for it near the 30 Corps Memorial.

TO ALL DESERT RATS WHO MARCHED FROM MERSA MATRUH TO BERLIN

A MARCH UNSURPASSED THROUGH ALL THE STORY OF WAR

May the fathers long tell the children about this tale! May your glory ever shine! May your laurels never fade! May the memory of this glorious pilgrimage of war never die!

Berlin, July 21, 1945   *Winston Churchill*

Foreword

General Sir John Mogg,
GCB; CBE, DSO

This book contains the second volume of 'The Desert Rats at War' and covers the final stages of the march of the 7th Armoured Division into Europe. This march, described by Sir Winston Churchill as "Unsurpassed through all the story of war", is vividly portrayed by George Forty and by so many of those who served in the Division who have contributed their experiences and memories.

The book will serve not only as a historic record of the Division's triumphant progress, but it has the advantage of describing the victorious path to Berlin in a simple, human, light-hearted, easy-to-read style, lavishly illustrated with excellent action photographs.

The question 'What was it like?' is difficult to answer after so many years. This record of first hand accounts, as seen through the eyes of the soldier, the NCO, the young officer and the senior officer does much to describe the 'feel of the battle', at the same time bringing out the characteristics of courage, staunch fighting spirit, light hearted comradeship, discipline, and devotion to duty and the Cause; all of which contributed to the indomitable spirit and professional ability of the Desert Rats.

Having served in the Division both in peace and war and with a son so recently in its successor, the 7th Armoured Brigade, it has given me great pleasure and immense pride to write this foreword and I hope that all who read this book will be inspired by the example of courage and proud achievement that it portrays.

General Sir John Mogg,
GCB, CBE, DSO.

John Mogg

General.

7

Introduction

As I explained in the introduction to my first book (*Desert Rats at War, North Africa*), I received such a tremendous flood of letters and offers of help from so many ex-Desert Rats that I was quite unable to compress everything within the covers of a single book without leaving untold and unseen many of the marvellous stories and photographs I had received. Fortunately my publishers felt the same way, so I have been able to divide the story of this unique Division into two volumes. Despite this extra space, however, I can still only highlight a small number of the momentous events which took place, in order to try to give the reader some idea of what it was like to be a member of the Division in action in Italy and North West Europe. I hope those who fought so gallantly in other Divisions will excuse the favouritism I am showing towards the Desert Rats, but I am in good company for did not the late Sir Winston Churchill call them his 'Dear Desert Rats' and go on to say that he hoped that 'the fathers would long tell the children of this tale'. So I am after all only doing as he asked.

I have started this second volume in Homs, where the Division rested and re-fitted after the Allies' great victory in Tunisia. Then, leaving their natural habitat in September 1943, the Desert Rats sailed across the Mediterranean to Italy as part of the American Fifth Army under General Mark Clark, landing at Salerno in early September 1943 just as Italy signed the armistice. After a brief, but exceptionally hard-fought campaign, they re-embarked at Naples, reaching the United Kingdom early in January 1944. There followed a period of hectic preparations for

Right: Christmas Broadcast, December 25th, 1944 – The Journey Back. Corporal Bob Pass of 1/5th Queens, one time Brixton window-cleaner, assisted by Frank Gillard, gets ready to deliver the Christmas Day message which was heard by the folks back home just before the King's address. It was entitled 'The Journey Back' and told the story of every soldier's hopes for the future. Afterwards Bob, who had served at Dunkirk, in Crete, Libya, Sicily and Italy, went on fighting with the Division deep into Germany. Surrender was near and the end of the war had become something one could think about in easy terms like days or weeks. Then on Sunday April 22nd, 1945, Corporal Bob Pass and a patrol flushed a group of Germans out of a wood. One raised a white flag and Bob went forward to meet him. As he did so the other Germans fired at him and he was mortally wounded. For Corporal Bob Pass there was alas no 'Journey Back'.

D-Day during which time the Division had to master a completely new tank, the Cromwell. As you will read there were some misgivings over this tank which many considered to be inferior to the Sherman they knew so well. In addition, the Division lost a large number of experienced officers and soldiers, sent to bolster up other Divisions who lacked the Desert Rats' battle experience. This must have caused General Bobbie Erskine many sleepless nights, especially as once again his Division was to be in the spearhead of the assault, as the first armour ashore at Arromanches.

After the almost limitless space of the Desert, the Division had to learn many new skills and in particular had to become accustomed to fighting within the constraints of close country and built-up areas. Some of these skills could only be learnt the hard way, as is evidenced by the bitter and bloody fighting in the bocage of Normandy. From then onwards the Division was virtually never out of action, in the forefront of the advance across Europe, which for them included such high spots on the way as the relief of Ghent and the surrender of Hamburg. It was fitting, therefore, that as 'first in and last out of the battle' they should be chosen to go to Berlin and there to take part in the great Victory Parade held in July 1945. The story of the Desert Rat does not end there

I'm glad to say, otherwise I might never have had the privilege of wearing one on my arm! And so I have tried to bring the story up to date, by including some brief reference to the post war years and to the Seventh Armoured Brigade, the natural successors of this great Division.

This Introduction is, I feel, a good place to record how indebted I am to the Ministry of Defence Library who have cheerfully allowed me to empty their shelves and to keep out their books for much too long. How lucky we are in the Services to be so well served by such a splendid library.

I must again thank Michael Haine for his excellent maps and diagrams, Mrs Nancy Rogers for her ever-smiling countenance and ever-efficient typing; Jon for once again allowing me to include his 'Two Types' and Giles for his own inimitable rendering of 'Dear Desert Rats'. To them and to all the other kind people who have given me so much help and encouragement during the months of preparation I offer my sincere thanks.

May the spirit of this great Division live for ever.

Floreat Jerboa!

George Forty
January 1976
Lulworth Camp, Dorset

Left: Longest Serving Member of HQ Seventh Armoured Division. The photograph, taken in January 1957, shows the late Captain 'Richie' Richardson, BEM, RTR, shaking hands with the then GOC, Major General J W Hackett (now General Sir John Hackett, GCB, CBE, DSO, MC). 'Richie' Richardson had a record any Desert Rat could be proud of, having served with Headquarters Seventh Armoured Division continuously since its formation in August 1939. A sergeant at the outbreak of war, he was promoted WO2 and then WO1 with the Headquarters and was recommended for an immediate commission in August 1943. However, he chose to remain in his job with the Divisional HQ and consequently was not commissioned until September 1945. Captain Richardson served with no fewer than sixteen different GOCs, a record which to my knowledge is quite unique.

Homs~The Division Relaxes

Probably the most well-remembered concert party to perform in the Leptis Magna amphitheatre included Vivien Leigh, Bea Lillie and Leslie Henson, seen here on the stage in August 1943.

Leptis Magna – A concert party in progress in the Roman amphitheatre of Leptis Magna, close to Homs.

The North Pole?

'I suppose we could have been put in a worse place than Homs, those I can think of off hand – the North Pole, Devil's Island or the middle of the Amazon jungles. It was a place with a population of perhaps two hundred, one main street with some lemonade shops and a few quite nice villas down by the sea. We were camped about five miles to the east on the shore. On the north side of the road there was a cultivated patch of palm trees, water melons, limes and beans of different sorts, with some huts scattered about. There was a track leading through this patch and from the edge of it to the sea about three hundred yards away – that is the place we lay all summer. Between the camp and the village lay the ruins of Leptis Magna'. (*Wardrop of the Fifth, Ed Major J. Garnett, MC*).

Jake Wardrop was perhaps being a little hard on the choice of Homs as the place where the Division would spend the three months before going to Italy. It certainly was better than Bou Arada, the Division's first stop after the capture of Tunis which was a wilderness with no sign of life apart from the odd cactus. Homs was at least close to the sea, with all the unit camps within walking distance of the

beach which made up for a lot. Almost everyone swam daily and by the time the Division left, there was hardly a non-swimmer to be found. Even Jake cheered up a bit and the next entry in his diary recalls: 'It was about the end of May and we were sitting at Homs. We still had our tanks, but had moved into Troop areas with tents, or if somebody had no tent he built a little shelter out of groundsheets and that kept the dew off at nights. I was in Headquarters Troop and we had four crews, less the officers, who all slept in an area together. Behind us was 11 Troop, Henry and Cliff; behind them was 9 with Snowy and Digger, and on the left were 10 with Joe and Ted and 12 with Jumbo and Bertie. In the middle was the cook-house and near it the Quartermaster's lorry. We ate together here as a squadron, sitting on the sand like wogs in the sun. Up on the edge of the cultivation, the fitters had built a hut of boards, galvanised iron and sheets. It was a great little shack, just like a beachcomber's hut on one of the islands. We did nothing for weeks but sit in the sun, swim, read and eat. At night we'd sit around listening to the wireless or go to Leptis to see a concert. There was some beer, most times two bottles per man, but there were always

some who didn't want it and Stan, George and I did miles running round to see who didn't. The Sergeants had a bottle of whisky occasionally and I bought Ted's as he didn't drink it and it came in handy. The first excuse for a party was the return of Dixie from South Africa, he had gone away sometime before. By good luck he arrived on a beer day and we had a nice little session that night. One day somebody had a brainwave, to build a Mess Room, so that we could sit down to eat. We got a few lorries and scoured the countryside for weeks and it was surprising how much there was. There was enough to build a cookhouse, dining room and a little Officers' Mess, so now we had our meals from a table sitting on a form, all our own work. One day we built a raft, it wasn't a huge success, but we had a lot of fun making it.'

The Jerboa Club

One amenity which was established at Homs, thanks mainly to the hard work and perseverance of the Division's Senior Chaplain, Kenneth Meiklejohn, was the Jerboa Club. It had opened very briefly in Tunis in what had been the German Legation, but on May 17th the furniture was loaded onto lorries and driven to Homs, as Kenneth Meiklejohn recalls:

'The furniture and other belongings of the club were loaded on to two or three 3-tonners, and left Tunis at 1300 hours on Monday, May 17th, 1943. We stopped at El Djem the next morning to look at the Roman amphitheatre, and my driver and I found later that we were infested with fleas as some of the tunnels had been used by the Bedouin. We reached Tripoli on the 20th where Peter Ashton told me what he had arranged at Homs, which we reached on the 21st and took over the Leptis Magna Hotel, the only sizeable building in the village. It was quite empty except for some headed writing paper and the hotel rubber stamp, but we had enough chairs etc to furnish the large main hall. We did in fact, open that evening. All we could offer were cups of tea, such magazines and papers as we could get, and a few things, cigarettes etc., either from the NAAFI or from a YMCA or Church of Scotland van which called on its way to Tripoli. "We" were three or four men and myself. We alone slept in the hotel, where I turned one room into an office and another into a chapel. The Club was open to all ranks – to the surprise of some officers from other Divisions who

A general view of Homs, taken from the roof of the Jerboa Club.

assumed it would be an "Officers Only" club. Every Sunday we had an evening Service in the hall, which was quite well supported. We also had a weekly Bible study group, Confirmation classes, meetings for such ordinands as could be traced, and two Toc H meetings (no lamp!)'.

The walls of the club were soon adorned with frescoes of tanks and armoured cars and, more important, of English countryside scenes and Arab dancing girls. There was also a cinema set up nearby and a 'Music for All' club was well supported.

Leptis Magna
The spectacular ruined amphitheatre of the old Roman town of Leptis Magna made a marvellous open-air theatre and was used for concert parties, church Services and other gatherings. The Army produced a leaflet on Leptis Magna which ended with these words: 'A great deal of work and money has gone to unearthing these remains for you to see. Please treat them carefully, watch where you tread in your army boots and if you must write your name, keep it for somewhere else!'

The Homs St Leger
One of the highspots of the rest period was a race meeting organised by 8th Armoured Brigade. The local sheikhs, who had been invited to take part, were delighted with the handsome presentation plaques made for the occasion by 8th Armoured Brigade Workshops. A tote, side-shows and a Sudanese band completed the 'all the fun of the fair'

atmosphere and the meeting was a resounding success.

Leave Parties

Leave parties were organised to Tripoli and Tunis as Jake Wardrop recalls:

'In the middle of June we started to run eight-day trips to Tunis, this was inclusive of time for the journey, so whenever a party went, they hammered the whole way only stopping for petrol, punctures and food. As soon as one driver got tired, another would take over, they'd go all night and there was a record for the trip which everybody tried to break. The distance was about seven hundred miles and the record, never broken, was twenty five hours, which wasn't bad for a three-ton Ford with fifteen in the back and maybe a blow-out thrown in.'

Main Problems Facing the Division

But it was not all recreation as three main problems faced the Desert Rats. First was the fact that the Division had to be completely re-equipped during the three months out of action. Second, individual training and in particular weapon training, had been neglected during the last few months of strenuous operations and had to be brushed up. Finally, the Division had to be trained for a completely different type of warfare in close country and also had to practise for their coming seaborne landing. Jake Wardrop recalls:

'About the beginning of August we started to equip again, the campaign in Sicily was drawing to an end and we all had a pretty good idea where we would be going next. The Highland Division had taken part, also 30th Division and the 4th Armoured Brigade. The tanks with big mileages were taken away and we got new ones, tracks were renewed and things started to move. I got a Sherman and the crew were Stan – driver, Carlo – machine gunner, Jimmy – 75mm, and old Pathan Woody – operator. We did some shooting and "Sure-Shot" Jimmy blew the targets to pieces at any range. All the old hands were there again. The ones who had sworn that they were finished after Tunis, the bugle blew and they were off to war. Henry and Cliff, Snowy, Digger, Dixie, Ted, Joe, "Slap Happy" Joe, who went to Head-quarters Squadron, and we had some pretty good officers. The Major, Captain Burt, Captain Boon and the commanders of 9, 10, 11 and 12, were Messrs. Heywood, Eckersley,

Osborne and Daniels. My old commander from Mareth was back and he was second in command of the Battalion.

Two chaps came from the REME one day and gave a demonstration of how a Sherman could be waterproofed to drive in six feet of water. They fitted a cowling over the air intake, extended the exhausts to stick up in the air, plugged everything up with putty and pitch and sealed down the driver's and machine gunner's flaps. It was then possible to drive in right up to the turret which they did one Sunday morning. We all turned out to cheer or laugh, depending on whether it was a success or not, and just in case, a tow rope was shackled to the tank on the beach. It was a huge success, the tank reversed right in until the water almost went into the turret, then came out forward. They did it once more for good luck and the experiment was over. Within a week all the tanks in the Battalion had been treated for taking to the

Top left: Good Bathing. The best feature of Homs was the bathing and most of the Division swam every day.

Centre left: The Jerboa Club. The Divisional sign which hung over the club entrance. The club, like all those established by the Division, was open to all ranks.

Bottom left: The ruins of Leptis Magna. Tripolitania, the Land of Three Cities, takes its name from the cities of Oea (the modern Tripoli) Leptis Magna and Sabratha. They were founded as trading stations by the Phoenicians some time before 500 BC. The Roman city belongs to two periods, the earlier dating back to the first century BC – hence the notice!

Below: Cover of the race card for the Homs St Leger Meeting, 29th August 1943.

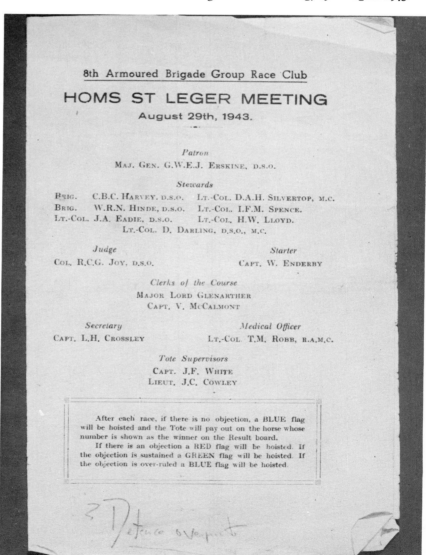

8th Armoured Brigade Group Race Club

HOMS ST LEGER MEETING
August 29th, 1943.

Patron
MAJ. GEN. G.W.E.J. ERSKINE, D.S.O.

Stewards
BRIG. C.B.C. HARVEY, D.S.O.   LT.-COL. D.A.H. SILVERTOP, M.C.
BRIG. W.R.N. HINDE, D.S.O.   LT.-COL. I.F.M. SPENCE.
LT.-COL. J.A. EADIE, D.S.O.   LT.-COL. H.W. LLOYD.
LT.-COL. D. DARLING, D.S.O., M.C.

Judge   *Starter*
COL. R.C.G. JOY, D.S.O.   CAPT. W. ENDERBY

Clerks of the Course
MAJOR LORD GLENARTHER
CAPT. V. McCALMONT

Secretary   *Medical Officer*
CAPT. L.H. CROSSLEY   LT.-COL. T.M. ROBB, R.A.M.C.

Tote Supervisors
CAPT. J.F. WHITE
LIEUT. J.C. COWLEY

After each race, if there is no objection, a BLUE flag will be hoisted and the Tote will pay out on the horse whose number is shown as the winner on the Result board.
If there is an objection a RED flag will be hoisted. If the objection is sustained a GREEN flag will be hoisted. If the objection is over-ruled a BLUE flag will be hoisted.

Left: Coming up the straight in the Homs St Leger. It was a five furlongs race for Arab ponies owned and ridden by local sheikhs.

Below: Homs St Leger – the Tote.

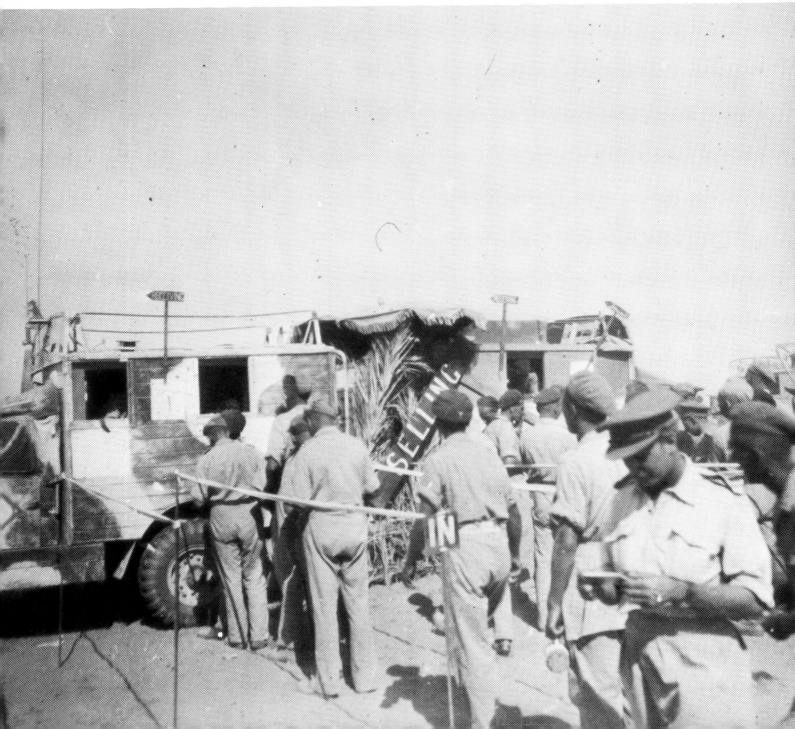

water except for some finishing touches which were to be done in the Tripoli area. We started to buy rations for the campaign, sausages, tins of steak and kidney, and all sorts of stuff like that. Below the turret the tool box was crammed full of tins, we hoped that at least we would get a chance to eat some. On August 27th the tanks were packed, the work was finished, we were ready to go. It was great, the lads were frisking around like dogs with two tails, our spirits had soared sky-high again. That day the canteen came again and by the old ruse Stan, George and I got five each of beer, which was better than nothing. We had a little party for a farewell to Homs, that delightful seaside resort.'

Visit of HM The King

Another of the highlights of the Division's rest period was a visit by His Majesty the King. Most troops had the opportunity of seeing him and the Eleventh Hussars, whose Colonel in Chief he was, had an informal visit all to themselves. Not long before *The Times* had described them as 'those incomparable paladins'.

Sicily

The Division was not used in Sicily although General Erskine, with a tactical headquarters, containing operations, intelligence, supply and medical representatives, did participate. The idea was that if there was a need to weld together the independent armoured brigades

Practising for the Invasion. A Sherman being backed onto a landing craft from a rocky North African beach.

in Sicily, then HQ 7th Armoured Division would assume control. As things turned out, however, this proved unnecessary and after about a fortnight the 'Tac' HQ became definitely and officially superfluous and had to return to Tripoli. The period had not been entirely wasted, however, some valuable lessons had been learned and to quote from the Division's official history: 'Sicily at that time of the year was not without its compensations, which included the sweetest and juiciest oranges known to man, sixteen varieties of Marsala and a gaggle of artistes from the Italian version of ENSA, one of whom had been endowed by Nature with scarlet hair and green eyes'.

Invasion of Italy

The main operation for which the Division was now preparing was of course the invasion of Italy. There were two schemes – one a landing down at the toe of Italy, the other, a bolder scheme, to land at Salerno with the object of capturing Naples. The Division first of all prepared to take part in the former – Operation 'Baytown' – the Eighth Army's landing in SW Italy, but was later switched to Operation 'Avalanche' – the Fifth Army's landing on the Gulf of Salerno. This meant that for the first time the Desert Rats were to come under command of an American Army, that of General Mark Clark. Planners soon found that they were grappling with 'bumf' on a lavish scale (known as 'Poop' by the Americans) and one staff officer was heard to enquire whether 'Avalanche' referred to the actual operation or the paper preceeding it!

Re-organisation and re-equipment

As well as taking every opportunity to enjoy themselves in the Homs area the Division, as has been explained, had much to do re-organising and re-equipping units. Every vehicle that could possibly be repaired was repaired, every wireless set was stripped, serviced and checked. Indeed the Workshops and Light Aid Detachments worked just as hard as they had done during the long months of desert operations. Most spares and new equipment had to come by road from the Delta, over 1 500 miles away, because all shipping was required for the invasion of Sicily.

There were no great changes in the equipment of units except in the case of the Divisional Armoured Car Regiment, the Eleventh Hussars, where each squadron was given an extra troop of White half-tracks in addition to their five armoured car troops. This troop combined the tasks of infantry and engineers to assist the Daimlers and Dingoes in their unceasing task of gathering information whilst following up the enemy as he withdrew. In addition, a formidable change had taken place to the Jeep Troop which had been replaced by a Gun Troop of two 75mm guns mounted on White half-tracks. Squadron Headquarters operated in three Humber armoured cars and a Dingo and an anti-aircraft gun section had been added to the B1 Echelon.

Order of Battle

For the invasion of Italy the Division was now organised into two brigades, one armoured and one infantry. It was to remain roughly in the same organisation for the rest of the war. The complete order of battle was:

22nd Armoured Brigade
1st Royal Tank Regiment (Equipped with Sherman Tanks)

Below: His Majesty, Colonel in Chief of the 11th Hussars inspects the regiment on June 21st 1943. (Left to right: Lt Col Smail, HM The King, General Erskine and General Montgomery).

5th Royal Tank Regiment (Equipped with Sherman tanks)

4th County of London Yeomanry – The Sharpshooters (Equipped with Sherman tanks)

1st Rifle Brigade (Motor Battalion)

131st (Queens) Brigade

1st/5th Queens Royal Regiment (Lorried Infantry Battalion)

1st/6th Queens Royal Regiment (Lorried Infantry Battalion)

1st/7th Queens Royal Regiment (Lorried Infantry Battalion)

'C' Company 1st Cheshire Regiment (Medium Machine Guns)

Divisional Troops

11th Hussars – Divisional Armoured Car Regiment

Divisional Signals

Royal Artillery

3rd Royal Horse Artillery

5th Royal Horse Artillery

15th Light Anti Aircraft Regiment, RA

24th Field Regiment, RA

65th (Norfolk Yeomanry) Anti Tank Regiment, RA

69th Medium Regiment, RA

146th Field Regiment, RA

Royal Engineers

4th and 621st Field Squadrons, RE

143rd Field Park Squadron , RE

Royal Army Service Corps

No 5, 58, 67, 287, 432 and 507 Companies, RASC

Royal Army Medical Corps

2nd Light Field Ambulance

131st Field Ambulance

70th Field Hygiene Section

21st Mobile Casualty Clearing Section

3rd Field Surgical Unit

7th Field Transfusion Unit

132nd and 135th Mobile Dental Units

Royal Army Ordnance Corps

Divisional Ordnance Field Park

Royal Electrical and Mechanical Engineers

22nd Armoured Brigade Workshops

131st Brigade Workshops

15th Light AA Workshops

Below: Gen Erskine, GOC 7th Armd Division, greets His Majesty, King George VI on his arrival to inspect the Division in June 1943.

Salerno

Salerno – View through the
windscreen of a Divisional
RASC vehicle soon after
landing.

EIGHTH ARMY

PERSONAL MESSAGE FROM THE ARMY COMMANDER

To be read out to all Troops

1. The time has now come to carry the war into Italy, and into the Continent of Europe. The Italian Overseas Empire has been exterminated; we will now deal with the home country.

2. To the Eighth Army has been given the great honour of representing the British Empire in the Allied Force which is now to carry out this task. On our left will be our American allies. Together we will set about the Italians in their own country in no uncertain way; they came into this war to suit themselves and they must now take the consequences; they asked for it, and they will now get it.

3. On behalf of us all I want to give a very hearty welcome to the Canadian troops that are now joining the Eighth Army. I know well the fighting men of Canada; they are magnificent soldiers, and the long and careful training they have received in England will now be put to very good use—to the great benefit of the Eighth Army.

4. The task in front of us is not easy. But it is not so difficult as many we have had in the past, and have overcome successfully. In all our operations we have always had the close and intimate support of the Royal Navy and the R.A.F., and because of that support we have always succeeded. In this operation the combined effort of the three fighting services is being applied in tremendous strength, and nothing will be able to stand against it. The three of us together—Navy, Army and Air Force—will see the thing through. I want all of you, my soldiers, to know that I have complete confidence in the successful outcome of this operation.

5. Therefore, with faith in God and with enthusiasm for our cause and for the day of battle, let us all enter into this contest with stout hearts and with determination to conquer.

The eyes of our families, and in fact of the whole Empire, will be on us once the battle starts; we will see that they get good news and plenty of it.

6. To each one of you, whatever may be your rank or employment, I would say:

**GOOD LUCK AND GOOD HUNTING IN THE
HOME COUNTRY OF ITALY**

B. L. Montgomery.

July, 1943.

*General,
Eighth Army.*

Salerno – Operation Avalanche

As I have explained, whilst Montgomery's Eighth Army was crossing the Straits of Messina to land on the toe of Italy, the men of the Seventh Armoured Division found themselves for the first time part of an American Army – the Fifth United States Army under General Mark Clark. The Fifth Army, which was to land higher up the Italian coast close to Naples in the Bay of Salerno, was composed of two Corps, one American (the 6th) and one British (the 10th). 10th Corps was commanded by General McCreery, who had recently taken over from General Horrocks when the latter was badly wounded in an air raid on Bizerta. He decided to use the two infantry divisions – the 46th and 56th (London) for the initial assault (see map), keeping 7th Armoured in reserve, ready to follow up and break out of the bridgehead once it was secured. Shortly before leaving North Africa General McCreery issued the following special order of the day:

SPECIAL ORDER

To be read to ALL Ranks of 10th Corps

We are now on our way to attack the Mainland of Italy. This decisive operation, in conjunction with the attack of Eighth Army in the toe of Italy, is the opening of the second front in Europe. Our landings will be a milestone in the downfall of Germany.

We form part of the American 5th Army. We shall be fighting and working alongside our American comrades, we must go all out to help each other. I have told General Clark how pleased all ranks of 10th Corps are to form part of an Allied force under his command.

We must expect hard fighting. Early success will depend largely on the speed of the initial landings and on the determination and dash shown by all ranks.

Throughout the world the British soldier has always been respected for his attitude to the civil population. We shall be in one of the most thickly populated districts of Europe. I rely on all ranks to make their conduct a model, and an example.

The 10th Corps forms the spearhead of the Army. I am very proud to be the Commander of such a splendid formation. Of the outcome I have no doubt. I wish you all good luck and God speed.

(Sgd) *R. L. McCreery*
Lt Gen
Commander 10th Corps

SUNNY ITALY

"Give me a sandstorm any day"

BOLOGNA 20 km.

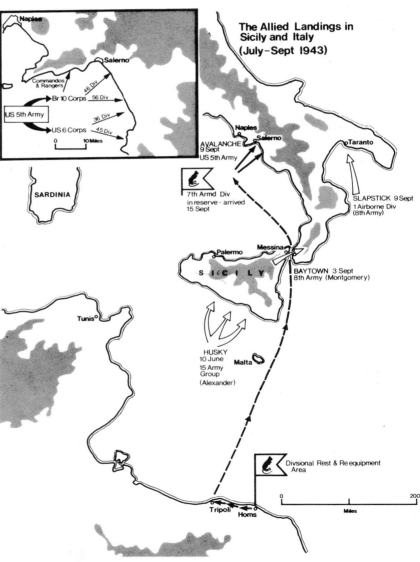

The Allied Landings in Sicily and Italy
(July–Sept 1943)

AVALANCHE 9 Sept US 5th Army

7th Armd Div in reserve - arrived 15 Sept

SLAPSTICK 9 Sept 1 Airborne Div (8th Army)

Taranto

BAYTOWN 3 Sept 8th Army (Montgomery)

Messina

Palermo

SICILY

HUSKY 10 June 15 Army Group (Alexander)

Malta

Divisional Rest & Re equipment Area

Tripoli Homs

Tunis

SARDINIA

Naples

Salerno

Commandos & Rangers

Br 10 Corps   46 Div   56 Div

US 5th Army

US 6 Corps   36 Div   45 Div

0   10 Miles

0   200   Miles

Far left, top: And so on to sunny Italy – but some Desert Rats preferred North Africa! (Reproduced by kind permission of Jon).

Left: Ready for Italy. Vehicles belonging to one of the brigade workshops lined up ready for loading at Tripoli docks.

Below: An Armoured Command Vehicle loading through the bow doors of a landing ship.

Left: Leaving North Africa. One of the landing ships passing wrecks in Tripoli harbour.

Right: Colonel (now Major General) Pat Hobart, the GSO1, briefs Divisional Headquarters personnel during the voyage to Italy.

Far right: The American captain of the landing ship which carried Divisional headquarters.

Below: Salerno, September 15th, 1943.

Salerno Beach. Generals Alexander, Mark Clark and McCreery survey the beachhead.

Final Preparation and Loading
Their final preparations made, the Division moved from Homs to Tripoli, where they boarded the landing ships which were to take them to Salerno.

First Desert Rats Ashore
Brigadier 'Bolo' Whistler, commanding 131 (Queens) Brigade, together with representatives of unit and brigade staffs, went ashore with the assault divisions, their task being to reconnoitre the proposed Divisional Concentration Area. They went in on September 9th, but surprisingly were not the first Desert Rats ashore as the following story from E. Mallas, a wartime member of 131st Field Ambulance explains:

'After the Division's great success in Tunisia, the 131st Field Ambulance were rested at Homs, east of Tripoli, near the ruins of Roman Leptis Magna. At the end of August 1943, ten volunteers were called for to take part in an "unknown" operation. I was one of those volunteers, who together with a "new to the unit" Medical Officer, set off along the coast road to Sfax, then on to Tunis and finally to Bizerta where we boarded an LCT (Landing Craft Tank) with our 15cwt Dodge truck and an ambulance,

eventually reaching Sicily where we were attached to the 41st Royal Marine Commando. On the same evening as we arrived a hurried departure was made in the middle of our preparations for the first real meal (American rations) we had had for days! Embarkation was followed by a voyage to the Italian mainland in another LCT, during which we heard the announcement of the armistice with Italy at 1800hours, September 8th. Late that same night we landed on the beach below the village of Vietri, on the road north of Salerno. I have now no knowledge of the date when the main body of the Division landed on the Salerno beaches, but 1 officer, 1 sergeant, 2 lance corporals and 7 privates of the 7th Armoured Division were among the first troops to land at Vietri, and like Horatio, to hold the bridge. At the first opportunity a Divisional Sign was drawn, coloured and hung from the balcony of the building for all to see who passed that way that the 7th Armoured were there before them. Our little "jaunt" brought one MC and one MM to the eleven Desert Rats, and one MM to the RASC driver of the ambulance'.

The Main Body Arrives
The main body of the Division started to

arrive on the evening of the 15th. They were expecting a hot reception as the BBC communiques, heard at sea, had talked about the sky over the beach area being 'dark with planes locked in mortal combat'. However, things were not quite as bad as that, although the situation was far from easy, as both the 46th and 56th Divisions had had some very tough fighting and the bridgehead was small and thinly held. The harbour of Salerno could not be used, whilst the town itself, like most of the bridgehead area, was under continuous enemy shellfire. Enemy counter attacks were numerous, but fortunately not properly co-ordinated. General Erskine's own White half-track broke a spring on its way to the concentration area and had to spend the night in a ditch, only to be chased out at 0400 hours the following morning during a spirited counter attack by 67th Panzer Grenadier Regiment – it withdrew at full speed with the sagging chassis tearing strips of rubber off the tyres!

The Advance Begins

After some anxious days the assaulting troops gradually began to gain the upper hand, helped by the continual pressure which the Eighth Army managed to put on the enemy from the south – they covered over 300 miles in seventeen days against considerable opposition, a remarkable achievement. By the 27th the Division was almost complete and the time had come for them to break out of the bridgehead. The plan was for the 46th Division to clear the pass through the mountains north west of Salerno as far as Camarelle. There the American Rangers would form a bridgehead through which the Division would pass, with 23rd Armoured Brigade under command. 23rd Armoured Brigade consisted at that time of only the Royal Scots Greys in Shermans, the King's Dragoon Guards in armoured cars, 24th Field Regiment less one battery, and one field squadron of sappers. The first objective was to be Scafati on the River Sarno. From there 23rd Armoured Brigade would advance straight on to Naples along the coast road, whilst the rest of the Division went north of Vesuvius and made for Capua on the River Volturno. The Division was unable to concentrate forward due to the close nature of the country and had to form up in line ahead behind the 46th Division. Due to the possibility of air attack the density of vehicles per mile was reduced to forty and at that spacing the Division covered no less than fifty-five miles of road – the distance from London to Brighton!

A knocked out German StuG III assault gun near Salerno. This low compact, self propelled 75mm gun had a top speed of 25mph and a crew of 4.

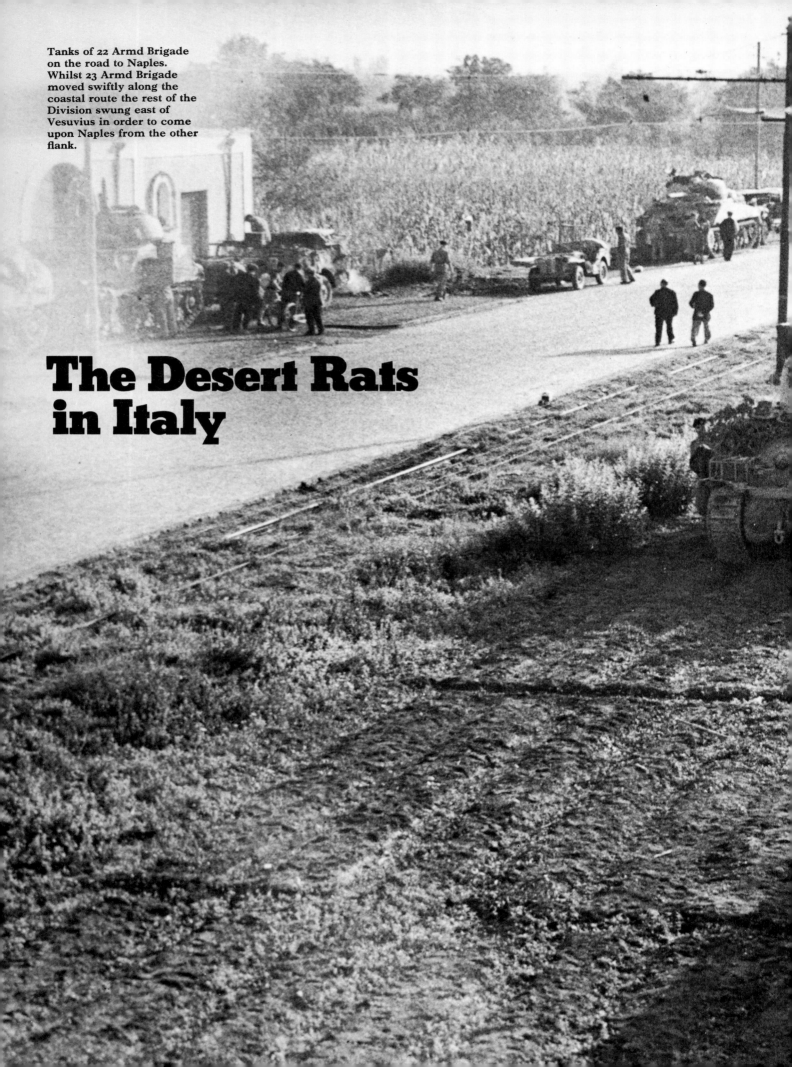

Tanks of 22 Armd Brigade on the road to Naples. Whilst 23 Armd Brigade moved swiftly along the coastal route the rest of the Division swung east of Vesuvius in order to come upon Naples from the other flank.

The Desert Rats in Italy

Although the Desert Rats were only in Italy for about three months, the campaign in which they fought was never an easy one. Italy had surrendered even before they arrived, but the German Army was still full of fight and conducted a masterly delaying battle as it slowly withdrew northwards. Crack Hermann Goering units faced the Desert Rats, their rearguard parties usually consisting of one or two self-propelled guns, protected by dug-in machine gun and rifle positions. An armoured car some distance in front of the main position would give timely warning of approaching British forces, whilst roads were mined or blocked with felled trees, and booby traps abounded. Artillery guns or 'Moaning Minnies' (Nebel-werfers) in depth would bring down accurate fire on anyone who advanced without due caution. Typical of the small but bloody engagements fought by the Division was the

Far left, top: A Sherman tank of the 1st Royal Tank Regiment passing an Italian farmer with his ox-drawn farm cart on the road to Aversa.

Far left, centre: 1/6 Queens enter Scafati. The battalion under Lt Col M Forrester was leading the Division and made a lightning dash for the main bridge over the R Sarno. It had been prepared for demolition and was guarded by the 2nd Herman Goering Panzer Regiment. The 1/6 Queens managed to capture the bridge intact and beat off all counter attacks.

Far left, bottom: An 11th Hussars Armoured Car enters Pompeii. After Scafati the Division made slow progress against skilful and energetic German rear-guards. Roads were mined and blocked by felled trees then covered by self-propelled guns, machine guns and rifle positions. Towards the end of September opposition lessened and the main body of the Division pushed on, led as usual by 11th Hussars patrols.

Above left: HQ 7th Armoured Division in the main square of Pompeii, Div HQ was never far behind the leading troops throughout the advance.

Left: A self-propelled Priest in action near Torre Annunziata. The US M7 'Priest' was equipped with a 105mm howitzer which was mounted onto a Sherman hull. The Priest seen here was supporting 23rd Armd Brigade in their thrust along the coast to Naples.

battle of the 1st Battalion of the Rifle Brigade at Cardito, a small town surrounded by thick vineyards and woods. The enemy had a number of self propelled anti-tank guns in the vineyards, protected by machine gun posts on the outskirts of the town. After some of 1 RTR tanks had been destroyed by these guns, the motor company working with them, C Coy, 1 RB, put in a spirited attack, but this proved unsuccessful and so the whole of the battalion had to be used.

Here is an account of the action as told by Major General Sir Victor Paley KBE, CB, DSO, DL who was then commanding the battalion:

'At the beginning of October 1943 the Division was engaged in an outflanking movement which entailed passing east of Vesuvius to get round behind Naples. On October 2nd, 22nd Armoured Brigade passed through the lorried infantry brigade and spearheaded the advance on two roads. On the right, 1 RTR with its motor company (C Coy 1 RB) under command, had just about reached Afragola, but the next morning the tanks were held up south of Cardito by unlocated enemy anti-tank guns well concealed in vineyards and standing maize. An attempt by the motor company to dislodge the enemy proved abortive, as on their start line the two motor platoons came under heavy shell fire probably directed by a concealed OP close at hand, and lost one third of their strength in casualties.

The Brigade Commander, to whose tactical headquarters that of my own was attached, then told me to recover my other company and take on the task of clearing the town, as 1 RTR had lost tanks both to the left and to the right of Cardito and could not get on. Recovering this company ("I" Company) which was away behind with 5 RTR took some time, as the platoons had been dispersed on reconnaissance tasks. Brigade Tactical HQ was located in the northern end of Afragola some two hundred yards from the main road which rather avoided the centre of the village. Immediately in front was a wood, widish at our end but tapering to a point at Cardito. There was the occasional airburst shell probably unobserved, a bit short, far too high and quite harmless. It was quite obvious that there was no future in attacking across the open ground on either flank, and that the wood was the only sensible approach, even though no real

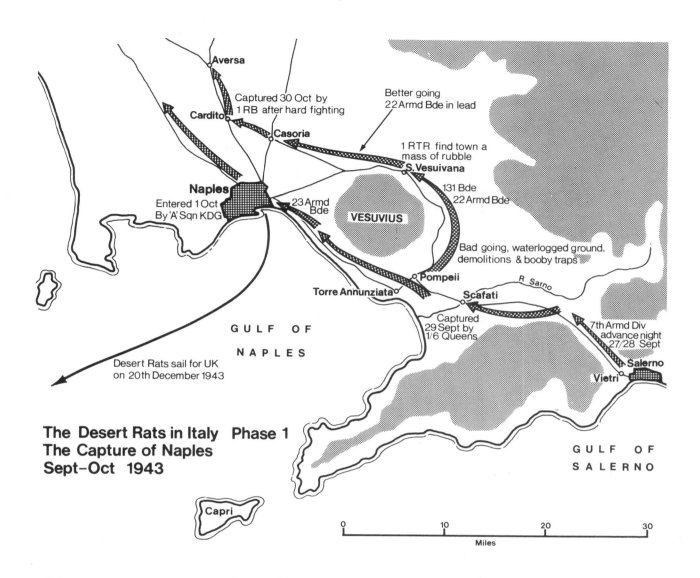

Aversa

Captured 30 Oct by
1 RB after hard fighting

Cardito

Casoria

Better going
22 Armd Bde in lead

1 RTR find town a
mass of rubble

S. Vesuivana

Naples

Entered 1 Oct
By 'A' Sqn KDG

23 Armd
Bde

131 Bde
22 Armd Bde

VESUVIUS

Bad going, waterlogged ground,
demolitions & booby traps

Pompeii

R. Sarno

Torre Annunziata

Scafati

GULF OF

NAPLES

Desert Rats sail for UK
on 20th December 1943

Captured
29 Sept by
1/6 Queens

7th Armd Div
advance night
27/28 Sept

Salerno

Vietri

**The Desert Rats in Italy   Phase 1
The Capture of Naples
Sept–Oct 1943**

GULF OF

SALERNO

Capri

0   10   20   30

Miles

Far left, top: Greys tanks
carrying men of the 1/6
Queens into Torre
Annunziata. A Sherman of
the Royal Scots Greys
loaded with men of 1/6
Queens, searching the
streets of Torre Annunziata
on the road to Naples.

Far left, centre: First KDG
armoured car into Naples.
At 0930 hours on October
1st, 1943, the leading
armoured car of A Squadron
of the King's Dragoon Guards
triumphantly entered Naples.

Far left, bottom: 4 CLY in
Casoria. The crew of a
Sherman tank of the
Sharpshooters carry out
their morning toilet with an
interested audience in the
background!

Left: 5 RHA OP in Arzano.
Captain Tacey of 5 RHA
mans an observation post
in a bell tower in Arzano,
bringing down accurate
fire on enemy positions.

reconnaissance could be carried out to see exactly what enemy posts it contained. I knew that the first 150 yards were clear as I had walked a little way into the wood and in any case all of us standing at the edge of Afragola would have been shot at if the enemy could have seen us. I made a plan with Peter Gregson (CO 5 RHA) to support the attack with a barrage. I forget the timings now but I know that the opening line got a double dose and was probably about 200 yards into the wood. The plan was largely made from the map and we were fortunate enough to have very accurate large scale maps.

When my other company arrived there was not all that much time left for giving out orders. Bill Apsey, who was commanding it, decided to go in on a one platoon front, which was sensible, as the wood tapered to a point. It was also fairly thick, so the riflemen were almost on top of the enemy posts (not

Right: GOC 7th Armoured Division, General Bobbie Erskine driving his jeep near Naples.

Below: A Divisional supply column moving towards Naples. Soon after Naples the network of roads increased so the armour could take the lead. Behind them the columns of supplies rolled on unceasingly.

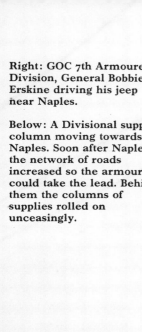

Right: The GOC receives a bouquet from the orphans of Casaluce. The Desert Rats earned the undying gratitude of this small town by organising transport to collect their most prized statue – 'The Silver Virgin of Casaluce' from nearby Aversa. The Aversans had borrowed it just before the Allied invasion and then boasted that because of the war they would be able to keep it for ever. But thanks to the 'Generale Magnifico' and his 'Liberatori Arditi' honour was satisfied. By the time the orphans had sung a very long anthem composed specially for the occasion, the sun had melted most of the chocolate General Erskine was carrying for them.

Centre right: 1/5 Queens in Aversa. A patrol searches the wreckage of a bombed train for possible snipers.

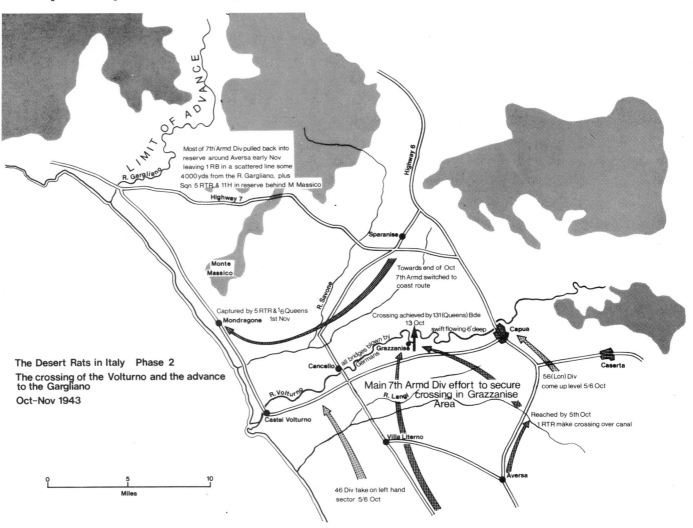

LIMIT OF ADVANCE

R. Gargliano

Most of 7th Armd Div pulled back into reserve around Aversa early Nov leaving 1 RB in a scattered line some 4000 yds from the R. Gargliano, plus Sqn 5 RTR & 11H in reserve behind M Massico

Highway 7

Highway 6

Sparanise

Monte Massico

R. Savone

Towards end of Oct 7th Armd switched to coast route

Captured by 5 RTR & 1/6 Queens 1st Nov

Mondragone

Crossing achieved by 131 (Queens) Bde 13 Oct

swift flowing 6' deep

Capua

all bridges blown by Germans

Grazzanise

Caserta

Cancello

56 (Lon) Div come up level 5/6 Oct

The Desert Rats in Italy   Phase 2

The crossing of the Volturno and the advance to the Gargliano

Oct-Nov 1943

R. Volturno

R. Lanol

Main 7th Armd Div effort to secure crossing in Grazzanise Area

Reached by 5th Oct 1 RTR make crossing over canal

Castel Volturno

Villa Literno

Aversa

0   5   10

Miles

46 Div take on left hand sector 5/6 Oct

that there were many of them as it turned out) before their occupants could use their weapons. The southern tip of Cardito was thus reached without much difficulty. The company then had to clear the village, a straggling place some seven hundred yards long – quite a task for a motor company which only had two motor platoons and only assaulted about 40 strong. As it turned out the actual clearing of the village was not too difficult and it was during the consolidation at the northern end that we had most of our casualties, as the enemy brought down some very heavy concentrations of fire at hourly intervals. There is no doubt that they had intended to hold their positions for several

hours at least until nightfall or possibly even for another day. And there was always the possibility of a counter attack. Things were not helped by electrical storms which put all our radios out of action for a period. It was impossible to locate the hostile guns until after dark when the medium regiment with the Division was able to silence the opposition and the Riflemen in Cardito got some relief. During the night the Germans broke contact and the advance was resumed the next day'.

Their Outstanding Feat in Italy
Thus, the attack and capture of Cardito was a complete success, indeed the Rifle Brigade considers it as their most successful engagement in Italy: As Major R. H. W. S. Hastings, DSO, OBE, MC says in his history:
'If Djebil Saikhra had been "I" Company's and possibly the Battalion's most successful battle in Tunisia, then the capture of Cardito was their outstanding feat in Italy. The company's attack on its narrow front was completely successful despite considerable opposition'.

Into Reserve
After reaching the River Garigliano in early November the Division was withdrawn into reserve behind the Massico feature, less 11th Hussars, 1st Rifle Brigade and a squadron of 5th Royal Tank Regiment, who took over a scattered line some four thousand yards

Above: 1/5 Queens practise for the crossing of the Volturno. By October 6th the country south of the R Volturno was clear of enemy. 46th and 56th Divisions had come up on the flanks of 7th Armoured and the stage was set for a crossing over the river. First, however, many preparations had to be made. The initial assault would be by infantry in small boats like these.

Left: A 2″ mortar in action on the northern bank of the Volturno. After ceaseless patrolling a suitable crossing place was found near Grazzanise and on the night of October 12th, 1943 elements of 1/5 and 1/7 Queens managed to cross. In the course of the next two days each battalion established a company on the far side.

Top left: An MMG of the Cheshires in action at the Volturno crossing. The medium machine guns of C Coy 1st Cheshire Regiment provided wonderful support to the Queen's Brigade during the crossing.

Centre left: A Sherman of 4 CLY crossing the river. Having bulldozed a gap on the far bank the tanks could now get across the river. At dawn on October 16th, 1943 the 1/5 and 1/6 Queens set out to clear the bridgehead as far as the canal some 2 000 yards north. A torrential downpour meant that the tanks which had crossed could only support this operation from the roads, but by nightfall the area had been cleared.

Bottom left: Sign on a pontoon bridge over the Volturno at Cancello.

Right: Gen Eisenhower talks with the GOC. The bridge over the Volturno which 7th Armoured Division sappers built at Grazzanise was the first across that river, so Gen Erskine has every reason for looking pleased as he talks with Gen Eisenhower.

Below: 1 RB mop up in Sparanise. Having crossed the Volturno the Division pressed on towards the next line of enemy resistance around Francolise and Sparanise and in the hills to the north. 1st Rifle Brigade entered Sparanise on October 22nd, 1943.

DEAD-SLOW YOU'VE BROKEN THE BLOODY BRIDGE ONCE

from the Garigliano. By the 7th however, all were withdrawn to the area of Aversa where they handed over their vehicles to the 5th Canadian Armoured Division. The official history, (*A Short History of the Seventh Armoured Division June 1943-July 1945.*), relates that the Canadians were a little surprised by some of the vehicles which had been with the Division since the previous February when they had been obtained secondhand from the 4th Indian Division. 'Several thousand miles, mostly over open desert had not subsequently improved them. However, all that could be done was done, and it was a misfortune that the crews who had worked so hard to freshen up tanks and vehicles as much as possible, should have had to hand them over in a field several inches deep in mud'

The Division then moved to concentrate on the northern side of the Sorrento Peninsula. Billets were reasonably comfortable and life agreeable as Jake Wardrop recalls:

'A day or two later some of the crew moved off down the coast to Sorrento and Castellamare and shortly after we drove the rest of the tanks to a dump in Napoli. It was a good trip. We waved to the signorinas and laughed when the lads on the pavements shouted that we were going the wrong way. Wrong way, indeed! On December 2nd the rest of the unit moved to Castellamare and we sat there for two weeks.

'C' Squadron was camped in a red jam factory which had been blown up by the Bosches, and a very good job they had made of it. I don't suppose the place will operate for months to come. It was a good spot and I met some people, quite a number. The first was a Canadian who could play the guitar and sing just like Jimmy Rogers. I met him in a wine shop and saw him again by chance one day on the road. One day I bought a guitar in a little shop, the one from Tunis had become a bit worse for wear. The owner of the shop was a lad called Antonio and he was a wizard on the guitar and mandolin. He invited me to come to his house any night and we could have a little jam session. His father and two brothers also played the strings and he had three sisters. One was married and living in Rome and they used to worry about her a lot. They also had some smashing gramophone records and we used to hear them often. I got a lot of instruction from Tony on the guitar and in Italian, too. They called me Giovanni and I went to dinner with them a few times. The cooks in the Squadron were

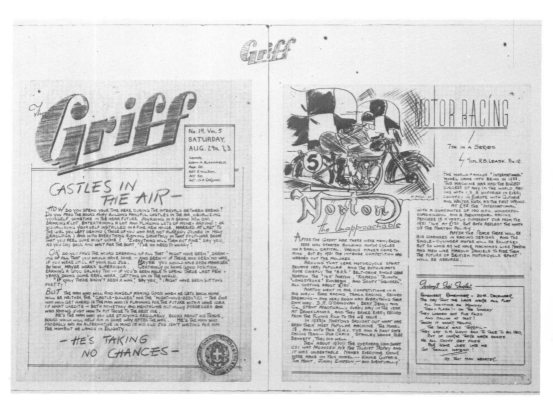

Above: A page from *Griff*, a POW newspaper published by ex Desert Rats in Camp No. 53, Macerata, Italy. Begun soon after their arrival at this camp, the newspaper was entirely hand written and hand drawn, six pages daily, it was a valuable morale booster for the inmates of the camp. After 15 months captivity Signalman Norman Bloomfield, the Editor, escaped with his two assistants and spent some 9 months fighting as guerillas until they were able to get through to the Allied lines.

Right: A Sherman of 1RTR fording a river near Mondragone. At the end of October 1943 the Division was moved south east to take over the line of the Regi Agena near the sea. They then pushed on northwards clearing Mondragone and occupying the Massico Ridge. It was by then bitterly cold and with enemy resistance hardening the Division fought its last action in Italy – a sharp engagement at Cicola.

continually weeping about the bread and rations that were missing every morning. I used to cane them, but what did it matter, we didn't starve and these people were hungry. I have their address and when I learn some more Italian and it is possible, I shall write to them. Nearby the 1st Tanks were staying in a big house and we visited them, then sent invitations to them to visit us. Many good nights were enjoyed by all and a lot of vino was consumed. There were some hospitals in the area and the personality kids, I mean the officers of 'C' Squadron, soon got chasing the nurses. One night I was coming back from the 1st, hazed a bit, guitar at the slope, jacket over one arm and had reached the door when Jock came dashing out and led me away to one side. He said there were some sisters in the Mess, so watch the language and so on. He was in quite a state. I got organised a bit and went in and there they were. Five English Sisters, looking clean and slick, sitting at the table. We sent out for ten bottles of vino and had a sing-song, it was very good'.

Going Home

Early on 20th December the Division, after a short night's rest in a wet and uncomfortable transit camp at Casoria, moved down to the docks of Naples to embark. By four o'clock, after spending most of the day in an almost stationary queue, all were on board and the

convoy weighed anchor. The voyage home was uneventful. Christmas and New Year were both celebrated fairly quietly, although the ships could scarcely have been described as "dry" except from the official point of view. On the 7th of January 1944, the Division docked at Glasgow where trains were already waiting to take the Desert Rats to their new concentration area in Norfolk. The short Italian campaign had at least given them a foretaste of what lay ahead and formed a useful transitional period between the Desert and the highly cultivated and urbanised battleground of North West Europe which was still to come. Jake Wardrop wrote in his diary aboard the boat home:

'The big job was finished and another one would be starting soon. We had done well in Italy and had the valuable experience of operating in continental conditions. That was the reason we did not come home after Tunis, we had to be introduced to the conditions of the continent, so different from the desert. And we had done so. We had learned some new tricks and improved on the old ones and now we were going home. There had been a lot of speculation about where we would dock, but I knew. I knew that morning when we got to the quay and I saw the ship, the Cameronia, and why not. I had set off from Princes dock and I'd go back there. It turned out that I was wrong by about a penny-one by tram; we landed at Shieldhall'.

Above centre: Handing over to the Canadians. 22nd Armd Bde workshops hand over a Sherman to their Canadian counterparts of the 5th Canadian Armoured Division. Conditions during this particular handover were better than for most of the units who had to contend with a sea of mud!

Above: Transit barracks near Naples. The Division spent a short night's rest in a rather wet and uncomfortable camp at Casoria near Naples before embarking.

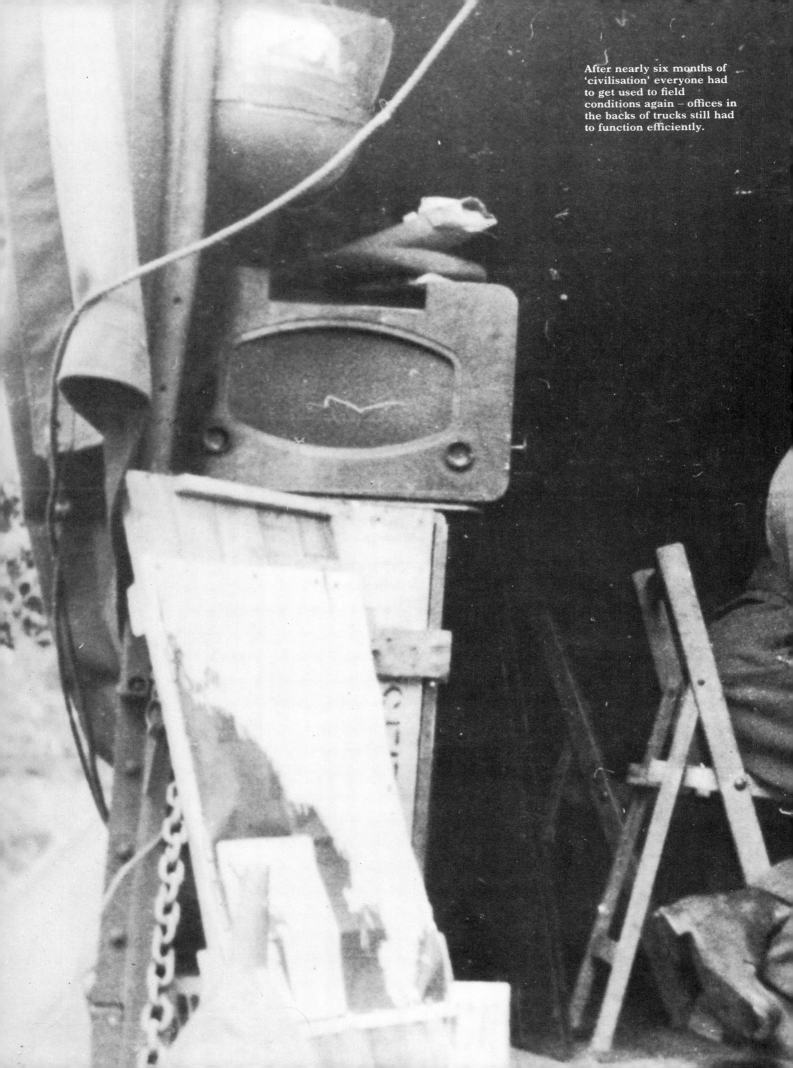

After nearly six months of 'civilisation' everyone had to get used to field conditions again – offices in the backs of trucks still had to function efficiently.

Blighty~Preparation for 'D' Day

Norfolk

The concentration area allocated to the Division was in Norfolk. The Queen's Brigade got the better choice of billets, being mainly quartered in civilisation around King's Lynn, but 22nd Armoured Brigade were around Brandon – not a particularly attractive area as the Divisional history relates:

'The Armoured Brigade was perhaps less fortunate in the Brandon area. Our misgivings had already been aroused by the publication of an article in *Country Life* which, while attributing to the district con-siderable importance for both archaeology and ornithology, made it clear that it possessed few, if any, other amenities. *Country Life* was right. Eager watchers, at the windows of the long troop trains, saw flat black fenland give way to sandy heath; Brandon station gave a glimpse at least of houses, and a pub; but the troop carrying vehicles into which we were detrained carried us inexorably away from this brief vision of paradise, farther and farther into the waste, depositing us mercilessly into groups of decayed Nissen huts, clustered beneath the tall pines. The 4th County of London Yeomanry were perhaps the most unfortunate, the greater part of their camp having been constructed well below the water level for the district, and they glared enviously at their neighbours, perched on their sandy islands above the waste. NCOs complained of the inadequacy of one hut for their platoons or troops; colour-sergeants enquired bitterly how they were expected to put the stores into "that there 'ole there" and deep inroads were made into the coal stocks before it was discovered that this commodity was, in England, severely rationed'.

Preparations for Normandy

Of course few really had much time to worry about their surroundings for there was a great

deal to do. The GOC, General Erskine, later wrote of those busy days:

'When the Division arrived in early January they had to have their leave. We then had to draw complete new equipment for the entire Division as we had left all our own in Italy. This in itself is a fairly major undertaking. It did not make matters easier when we found that the Armoured Brigade was to be equipped with Cromwells which was an entirely new tank for us. We all knew the Sherman inside out, but none of us knew the Cromwell. This had various repercussions. The Armoured Regiments had to learn the gunnery and maintenance of a new tank which many of them judged inferior to the Sherman. Many of the Cromwells suffered from minor defects and the reputation of the tank did not improve as we had to repair the defects ourselves. The Armoured Regiments all had to go to Scotland (Kirkcudbright) to do their gunnery which was absolutely necessary, but took up much time on a form of training which could have been avoided if we had been given Shermans.

At this time we were also very busy "planning". The enormous amount of detail required in this planning involved most of my staff and the brigade staffs. For a period of several weeks the senior members of my staff lived in London with 30 Corps planning staff. Matters were not made easier for me by the removal of Brigadier Whistler, commander of 131 Brigade to a brigade in 3rd Division. My GSO1, Lieutenant Colonel Pat Hobart, was taken to boost the Guards Armoured Division and my OC Signals was also taken away. A number of other valuable officers were taken away to boost other armoured divisions and divisions for the assault.

Our role was the immediate follow up of the assault and we had to commence our landing on the evening of D-Day. Naturally we paid a good deal of attention to landing in face of opposition. We could not rely on the assault being entirely successful and we had to be prepared, as much as an assault division, for landing in the face of opposition over beach obstacles. This required careful rehearsals with the Navy both in the proper loading of the LSTs (Landing Ships Tank) and in their disembarkation either direct on to the beach or onto large rafts. The tanks and all other vehicles had to be carefully waterproofed as we had to anticipate a "wet" landing. A tremendous amount of hard work and training was involved in all this which other armoured divisions did not have to undertake as they came to Normandy much later and could assume a "dry" landing. Therefore much of the training time available was spent

Top left: Mon Repos. In May 1944 units were moved from their Norfolk concentration areas to complete waterproofing, 22 Armd Bde to Ipswich and 131 Bde, plus most of the supporting arms, to the London docks area. Camps were mainly tented, like this desirable residence belonging to Maj A H Barnes of 7th Heavy Recovery Section REME, near Southampton.

Above: General Montgomery inspects the Division. Monty visited every unit of the Division on February 16th and 17th, 1944. Here he inspects 3 RHA. Lt Col Norman (then CO 3 RHA) is standing next to him, Brig Mews (Commander, Royal Artillery) and Gen Erskine (GOC) are next behind.

we had come from Italy where we had plenty of experience in working in close country. I should of course have welcomed a longer time to train. I am sure we all felt we were rushed, but bearing in mind the number of different things we had to do we gave as much time as we possibly could to field training in close country. I never for one moment felt I was taking to Normandy an untrained Division. I had the greatest confidence in them.

Morale was as always a very important factor. The Division contained many people who had been in it since 1941, who had seen the North African campaign through and had done Salerno. There was undoubtedly a feeling amongst a few that it was time somebody else had a go. I had to pay considerable attention to this attitude and I am sure I did so successfully, but it meant several heart-to-heart talks with every unit. There was a fundamental difference between troops like 7th Armoured Division who had been fighting continuously and fresh troops who had never been in action. The latter wanted to "win their spurs" and were ready to take on anything without question – once or twice. With 7th Armoured Division it was no use trying to pull the wool over their eyes. They knew war too well to take it light heartedly or carelessly. We left for Normandy with a high state of morale, but it is no use concealing the fact that we felt we had been rushed. We were nothing like so well teamed up as we had been before Salerno'. (Taken from the private papers of the late General Sir George Erskine and published by kind permission of Major P. N. Erskine.)

New Recruits

The Division received their quota of new recruits to make units up to strength. Some of these had most interesting backgrounds as the following reminiscences from R. Parker of London recall:

'Let me first introduce myself. I was born a German Jew and came to this country as a refugee in March 1939, aged 24. When war broke out we – that is countless young German and Austrian Jewish refugees – volunteered at once to fight Nazi Germany, in any capacity. The British Government eventually agreed to let us serve in the Army, but only in the Pioneer Corps. Some of the "alien" pioneer companies went to France with the BEF – I went as well – and we were amongst the last evacuated back to Britain in June 1940. From then onwards the pressure,

Above: The GOC inspects 8th Hussars. General Bobbie Erskine inspected the 8th Hussars at West Tofts, Norfolk on May 11th, 1944. He is seen here being greeted by the CO, Lt Col Goulburn. 8H were equipped with Cromwell tanks – seen in the background. The Cromwell VII usually mounted a 75mm gun, but can you spot the short barrelled 95mm? Two of them were in each Squadron Headquarters.

in the technicalities of an assault landing.

The time available was extremely short. I have no access to dates, so I speak from memory. Working backwards we had to embark our tanks on June 2nd and 3rd in Force S at Harwich – this was my own HQ and the 22nd Armoured Brigade Group. We had to be in our concentration areas some ten days before this and again before that we had to have all our kit packed and vehicles loaded and waterproofed. There were thus no opportunities for training after the beginning of May. In the end it worked out that we had about two weeks in the Stanford battle area to train and that is a very small area to exercise an armoured division. At the same time especially from the younger members of the "alien" pioneer companies, to join fighting units continued to no avail. The disinclination of the War Office to employ what were, after all on paper anyway, enemy nationals is understandable. Perhaps the significance of what it meant to be a Jew in Germany had not yet sunk home in this country. But as the war went on and application after application to fight went to the authorities, gradually the official attitude changed. I think that it was in some of the first Commando raids (St. Nazaire etc) that ex-Pioneers were fighting bravely and also some became casualties. Finally in 1943 there was a complete turn about by the War Office. Everybody who wanted to could apply for a transfer to a fighting unit. Some of the boys – but very few – went for the most glamorous undertakings – Commandos, Airborne, or were dropped as spies over occupied Europe. (In this last category, an old friend of mine in 93 Coy, Pioneer Corps even lived to tell the tale of a year as a wireless operator in wartime Southern Germany). The Infantry held little attraction, some went for the Gunners, but the bulk of transfers were to the Royal Armoured Corps. So it was that in the autumn of 1943 the RAC Training Regiments in Farnborough and Barnard Castle had for some weeks almost entirely ex-Pioneer Corps "aliens", as new intakes. By the time our training had finished, it was 1944 and it now so happened that 7th Armoured Division arrived in this country from Italy and its regiments were scattered over Norfolk, mainly in the Thetford area. The Division wanted reinforcements, and we had just finished our training, so the major part of the new RAC recruits, all alien ex-Pioneers, went to the armoured regiments of the Division in bulk. What the exact numbers were I don't of course know, but I estimate it was about 80 to 100. Most of them went to 8th Hussars and 1st RTR. Some to 5th RTR and some to HQ 22nd Armoured Brigade and HQ 7th Armoured Division. I myself was lucky enough to be posted to Divisional Headquarters, where I finished the war, without a scratch, in "Tac" – Divisional Tactical Headquarters Tank Troop (for the close protection of Tac HQ). Many of my former friends, however, were not so lucky. I personally know of Troopers Sandford, Richmond, Franklin and Jacobi in 1st RTR, who were killed in the first few weeks in Normandy. Others in 8th Hussars, including my good friend Tommy Halford, also fell in

Normandy or were wounded. One Trooper Marshal, was wounded and then taken prisoner by the Waffen SS, and spent a year as a POW in Germany, without any of his British mates giving him away to his captors (and his English was strongly accented). You will notice that we all served as troopers only. It was hardly to be expected to get promoted in a division as battle-hardened as 7th Armd by the time we were allowed to join. Let me add that my relations with my British comrades were perfect. I have never heard of any of my foreign comrades who did not integrate completely with their crews, many of them regulars and veterans of all the Desert battles. The fact that so many "aliens" were in the Division at the time was not well known to everybody. I heard officers in Div HQ in Norfolk remark about the amazing fact that teutonic accents could be heard in the 8th Hussars lines! Colonel Carver, as he then was, took a mate of mine in his own jeep to say a Jewish prayer over the grave of a fallen trooper in a Recce tank of 1st RTR. When I got demobbed in February 1946 and found myself an alien again in Civvy Street, General Lyne personally intervened for me at the War Office and saw to it that I became a British naturalized national at once. Of course all our names are not the ones we were born with. The War Office changed all those in 1943, even our original army numbers were changed. It certainly was a help to Trooper Marshal when the SS took him prisoner'.

Top left: Three Cheers for Monty! Characteristically Gen Montgomery spoke to every unit he visited. He always considered it essential to let the troops under him know what was going on and what he expected of them. This he started as commander of the Eighth Army and continued to do as C-in-C 21st Army Group.

Above: General Erskine talks to the Signals Troop of the 8th Hussars. Every armoured regiment had specialist personnel attached to it from other Corps, such as these signallers. As well as the GOC, the C-in-C and His Majesty the King, the 8th were visited by General Skliaron the Russian Military Attaché. He noticed their battle honour for the Crimean War and remarked upon it – things could have been difficult, but when he discovered that the regiment celebrated the 'Charge of the Light Brigade' at Balaclava every year, he remarked that the Russians did likewise which caused much laughter!

Above: Leaving for the docks. Having completed their waterproofing and made all other preparations, units were moved down to the docks to embark – the armoured brigade in LCTs (Landing Craft Tank) the rest in LSTs (Landing Ship Tank) and Liberty Ships.

Bottom right: A line of tank transporters belonging to 7th Heavy Recovery Section look strangely out of place in a peaceful English country lane.

Visitors and Inspections

The Division was once again honoured by a visit from His Majesty on February 24th, 1944. An eyewitness of his arrival in one location was Mrs Jessie Jary of Attleborough, who happened to be near the station just as the Royal train arrived. She writes:

'His Majesty the King visited a small company of the 22nd Armoured Brigade who were stationed at Attleborough and were drawn up on the platform at Attleborough station early one morning, it was a very well kept secret. I was going shopping and walked through the gates just as the Royal train drew in. I watched the King speak to the troops and was so close I could have touched him when he came to the end of the platform. I will always remember the nice smile he gave me as he passed'.

General Montgomery was of course another visitor as the photographs in this section recall. General Erskine visited all his units on numerous occasions. Amongst them were some new arrivals, for example, the 8th Hussars who had replaced the 11th Hussars.

The Eighth were an Armoured Reconnaissance Regiment which meant they were equipped very much like an Armoured Regiment, but without any heavy armament and with more than the normal complement of light reconnaissance vehicles. In fact the Eleventh rejoined the Division very soon after D-Day and the Eighth functioned as a fourth armoured regiment within 22nd Armoured Brigade rather than in a reconnaissance role.

Final Preparations

W. F. Halford of Norwich recalled the final period of preparation thus: 'A few weeks later we moved to High Ash, we were camped in the fir woods out of sight and spent most of the time waterproofing our vehicles. There was no leave, but I well remember on several occasions riding my motor-cycle between the trees, coming onto the road well away from the main guardroom and off home to Norwich for the night'.

All over Southern England the invasion forces readied themselves for the coming

SUPREME HEADQUARTERS
ALLIED EXPEDITIONARY FORCE

Soldiers, Sailors and Airmen of the Allied Expeditionary Force!

You are about to embark upon the Great Crusade, toward which we have striven these many months. The eyes of the world are upon you. The hopes and prayers of liberty-loving people everywhere march with you. In company with our brave Allies and brothers-in-arms on other Fronts, you will bring about the destruction of the German war machine, the elimination of Nazi tyranny over the oppressed peoples of Europe, and security for ourselves in a free world.

Your task will not be an easy one. Your enemy is well trained, well equipped and battle-hardened. He will fight savagely.

But this is the year 1944! Much has happened since the Nazi triumphs of 1940-41. The United Nations have inflicted upon the Germans great defeats, in open battle, man-to-man. Our air offensive has seriously reduced their strength in the air and their capacity to wage war on the ground. Our Home Fronts have given us an overwhelming superiority in weapons and munitions of war, and placed at our disposal great reserves of trained fighting men. The tide has turned! The free men of the world are marching together to Victory!

I have full confidence in your courage, devotion to duty and skill in battle. We will accept nothing less than full Victory!

Good Luck! And let us all beseech the blessing of Almighty God upon this great and noble undertaking.

Dwight D Eisenhower

onslaught. In May the Division moved to its concentration areas – 22nd Armoured Brigade to Orwell Park near Ipswich, the remainder to Brentwood and West Ham.

Order of Battle

The D-Day orbat of the Division was as follows:

22nd Armoured Brigade
1st Royal Tank Regiment
5th Royal Tank Regiment
4th County of London Yeomanry (The Sharpshooters)
1st Battalion the Rifle Brigade (Motor Battalion)
131st (Queens) Brigade
1/5 Queens Royal Regiment
1/6 Queens Royal Regiment
1/7 Queens Royal Regiment
No 3 Support Company, Royal Northumberland Fusiliers (Medium Machine Guns)

Divisional Troops
8th Hussars
Divisional Signals
Royal Artillery
3rd Royal Horse Artillery
5th Royal Horse Artillery
15th Light Anti-Aircraft Regiment
65th Anti-Tank Regiment (The Norfolk Yeomanry)
Royal Engineers
4th and 621st Field Squadrons
143rd Field Park Squadron
Royal Army Service Corps
Nos 58, 67 and 507 Companies
Royal Army Medical Corps
2nd Light Field Ambulance
131st Field Ambulance
29th Field Dressing Station
70th Field Hygiene Section
134th Mobile Dental Unit
Royal Army Ordnance Corps
Divisional Ordnance Field Park
22nd Armoured Brigade Ordnance Field Park
131st Brigade Ordnance Field Park
Royal Electrical Mechanical Engineers
7th Armoured Troops Workshop
22nd Armoured Brigade Workshop
131st Brigade Workshop
15th Light Anti-Aircraft Workshop
Royal Armoured Corps
No 263 Forward Delivery Squadron

The Great Crusade was about to begin!

A view of the Convoy. The
Allied Army comprised over
3½ million men, nearly
150 000 of which were to be
put ashore on D Day alone.

Invasion

Close-up of the deck of a Landing Ship Tank en route for France. The force assembled for the invasion was gigantic and included over 4 000 landing craft and 1 600 ancillary and merchant ships.

Embarkation

The shipping plan was that the armoured brigade, less its motor battalion, would sail in assault landing craft, aiming to land on D-Day or D + 1, whilst the infantry brigade, the operational section of the echelons and the bulk of the headquarters, were to sail in Liberty ships and coasters. General Erskine recalled after the war how the plan had to be modified:

'The Division embarked from a number of different points. I went round to see them all and also units of 50th Division and 4th Armoured Brigade with whom I was likely to have to work closely on arrival at the other side. 22nd Armoured Brigade and my own Tactical HQ embarked on LSTs (Landing Ship Tank) in the River Orwell at Dovercourt. The rest of the Division embarked in Troop transports mostly at Tilbury. The salient point was that the 22nd Armoured Brigade went very light in transport and supporting arms (infantry, gunners and sappers) and there was a considerable time lag before the rest came along from Tilbury and elsewhere.

We had a lot of difficulty at Dovercourt in loading the LSTs according to the tables. Many of the vehicles were extremely awkward articulated vehicles for preparing airfields – scrapers, bulldozers and the like. They were towed equipment and difficult to load backwards into an LST. We had all practised

loading but none of the drivers of these most awkward equipments had been given a chance. They nearly drove us mad and we got further and further behind in our loading schedules. Eventually Admiral Parry and myself had to scrap the programme and make one which could be carried out. Undoubtedly this earth moving equipment was necessary but it was a great embarrassment at such an early stage.

Those of us who embarked at Dovercourt collected into a convoy off Deal during the afternoon and evening of June 5th. We set forth during the night and passed through the Straits of Dover in the early hours of June 6th. We expected to receive salvos from France as we went past, but not a shot was fired. It was a bright and sunny day with a bit of wind and the sea flecked with white. It was not rough but the sea was in movement. We passed along the south coast without incident and after mid-day we began to meet LCTs and other small craft returning. The BBC was in full blast giving all the news and things seemed to be going well. This was good and in contrast to our arrival at Salerno where everything was going very badly while we were at sea. We were a large convoy and as we went westwards we joined up with other shipping. As we got off the Normandy coast the whole sea seemed to be ships. Nobody was attacked from the air or sea. It was all most orderly, except from our own bombardment

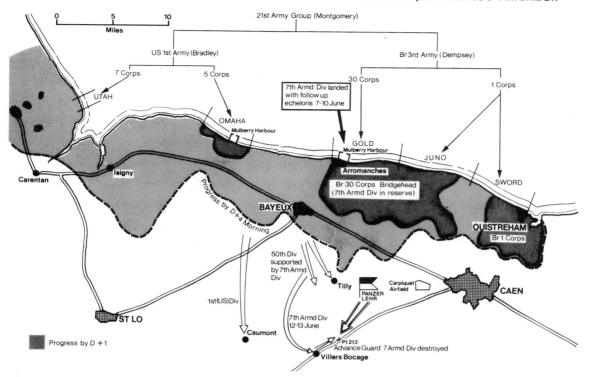

and bombing on the Normandy coast by the RAF, which increased as we moved to our positions opposite our beaches. We were in the vicinity of the beaches by the evening of D-Day, June 6th, and had anticipated landing on the tide about 2200 hours.

Very few people in our convoy landed on the 6th because the rough weather had "broached to" many of the early landing craft and the beach organisation could not handle us at the rate we were arriving.

Every LST was urgently required to do a return journey. It would have been far easier from our point of view to have sailed straight on to the beaches and unloaded. The objection to this was that the LSTs would have then lain on the beach stranded until the next tide floated them off and in the meantime they would have been 'sitting targets. Therefore, in theory, we were supposed to unload onto large floating platforms called Buffaloes and be towed in. It was just too rough for these Buffaloes; we could load on to them but they were too clumsy to move about. A good deal of time was wasted trying to make use of these things. Ultimately Admiral Douglas Pennant scrapped that method and ordered the ships ashore at half tide on the June 7th. I should think that was about 1100 hours. From the time of arrival we were champing at the bit to get ashore and particularly so from first light when we could not understand what was stopping us

driving straight on to the beaches. When the time came we plunged into the water and drove ashore without any trouble. The waterproofing worked splendidly and directly we reached dry land we unwaterproofed ourselves according to the drill. This involved a number of things including the blowing of a "cortex" charge when was an engineer invention to achieve a quick release. It was most effective but damaged the beer and whiskey reserve carried by some people on the sides of their tanks!' (General Erskine's private papers.)

Tanks Landing on Gold Beach
Gold Beach was the chosen beach for those units of the Division landing on June 7th. As Powell Jones of 4 CLY recalls at least one tank driver had his problems:

'At the Normandy landing on D + 2, we reckoned on driving off the tank landing craft into about 3-4 feet of water, but owing to rougher conditions and heavier swell, drove off into around 6 feet or so – a very strange sensation for the driver as all he could see through his visor was dark-green. Despite the strict instructions we'd received – "Keep your foot down on the accelerator, do not change gear, and drive straight ahead", one of the tanks in our troop drove out to sea! The last we saw of it was the sea up to the top of the turret and crew standing on the

Right: A section of a
Mulberry harbour on its way
to the beaches. Most landings
were initially made across
open beaches until
breakwaters could be
established by sinking block
ships. On Gold and Omaha
beaches enormous
prefabricated harbours,
known under the code-name
of Mulberry were
constructed. The vast steel
and concrete sections were
towed across the Channel
and then sunk off the
beaches.

Above: A destroyer shepherds the convoy towards the invasion beaches. Over 1 200 warships, including seven battleships and 23 cruisers, protected the great armada.

Below: The Convoy steams majestically on. This photograph shows clearly the small barrage balloons which were attached to all landing craft as a protection against low level air attack. As it turned out there was little enemy air interference as the Allied Air Forces had already crushed the Luftwaffe's fighter strength.

top looking quite forlorn. They rejoined the squadron a couple of days later with another tank – I think somebody got another rollicking over that one!'

Personal Impressions of the Landing
What was it like to be a member of that historic invasion force? The following account written by a soldier of the Eleventh Hussars gives one a graphic impression of their feelings on that memorable day:
'Our column moved off down the road to the loading area just before first light. A few hours' sleep in a very ordinary English ditch, the sight of stolid policemen at every side-

road, the thought of people still in bed and the early hour of the morning did not increase our morale. The loading onto the LCTs was accomplished surprisingly quickly and soon the craft were anchored in pairs in the middle of the estuary. From now on we had had it. No one could go ashore, no wireless was allowed and no newspapers came aboard. Movement was very limited, as to get from one end of the craft to the other it was necessary to crawl over the armoured vehicles.

After everyone had been organised into parties to cook and clean, there was nothing left to do but sit and wait; luckily the weather was good enough for sun-bathing. Amusement was provided by the small balloons attached to each craft, as in the strong wind they careered about until they got entangled with each other and then broke loose, gaining height rapidly until they burst when nearly out of sight. We thought that we should leave the next morning. Rumours went around for a time, but they soon ceased, as there was no scope for them amongst only forty people. We did not start the next morning, so had to settle down to another long day. The balloons had been tamed and, apart from sleeping, the only thing to do was

Top: A Sherman Firefly (17 pdr) belonging to the 4th County of London Yeomanry landing in Normandy. Over 320 000 men and 54 000 vehicles were landed in the first week.

Above: A column of waterproofed Sherman tanks, followed by some lorries, comes ashore through the shallows. By June 11th the Allied bridgehead was 50 miles wide by 12 miles deep.

to inspect the special rations which had been issued for use on landing. Self-heating tins of cocoa which brewed up in five minutes after being set off with a match won high praise. The weather was still good and we were lucky, as there was no shelter aboard and everyone had to sleep on the top of their vehicles or underneath them.

The following morning orders were given to pull the camouflage nets across the vehicles and interest began to rise as the craft prepared to move. Soon about fifty craft, in good order, were passing out into the open sea, which after the calm of the river seemed quite rough. Now we were definitely off and our thoughts were divided, some thinking of what was left behind, others of what they were going to, and a few too occupied to think, being ill over the side. The rest of that day was spent in readjusting ourselves to the motion of the boat, holding on to things when moving about, thinking twice before eating, and getting used to the spray which periodically dampened our ardour. Other convoys were seen, distinguished in the distance by the balloons each craft carried.

All seemed to be going different ways and nothing indicated any special direction.

The night was uncomfortable and there was also the thought that the Calais guns might open up. However, we heard nothing of them, though we learnt afterwards that a later convoy was engaged. At first light we were just in sight of the Sussex coast at the same time as the first troops were landing in France. A wireless set was opened to get any news that came over the Army broadcasts, but nothing was heard. As the day progressed so more convoys were seen, all converging, and now all were going in the same direction. Later still the craft could be seen stretching in four lines to the horizon in both directions. Naval launches were moving up and down the lines shepherding the craft into position. In the distance on either side escort vessels could be seen guarding the lane down which all the landing craft were moving. Planes in formation kept passing overhead at a great height. The balloons shining in the brilliant sun showed up like silver pin-heads on the horizon.

In the afternoon another wireless set was opened up on to the frequency of the infantry division which was landing in front of us. Soon we were getting the locations of the forward troops and it was with great satisfaction that we could mark on our maps a red line showing that the infantry had achieved a substantial bridgehead. Throughout the day the columns of craft had been moving at the same speed and without any checks or alarms. There was no sign of the German Air Force. Later in the evening the order was given to roll back the camouflage nets and to run the vehicle engines for twenty minutes. Then the shackles securing the vehicles to the deck were released and all precautions taken to ensure that the vehicles would not move, as the sea was still rough enough to make the motion of the craft unpleasant. Final adjustments to the waterproofing of the vehicles were made.

After the last meal had been finished and all kit had been stowed away, there was nothing left to be done but to sit on the vehicles and wait for the outcome of the operation which had been planned for years. As the sun went down more and more ships could be seen spread over a large area in front of us, the smaller ones moving forward and the larger ones at anchor. Everything was very quiet except for the engines, and it all gave an impression of a naval review rather than an operation to defeat the Huns for all time. As we approached the mass of ships, the lines of landing craft slackened speed and it seemed now that we should not land that evening. The craft moved slowly forward and just before light failed the shore could be seen, but only as a dark, long line, and nothing could be made out except for a few fires burning. There was no thought of sleep, because we knew that, though the Luftwaffe had not appeared during the day, they would certainly come that night. Tin hats that would fit were put on and everyone sat listening while the gun crews prepared for action. Attacks came at about hourly intervals throughout the night, but only by a few planes. The amount of metal that was shot up into the air was staggering, ranging from the heavy stuff from cruisers to the small stuff from individual weapons, and the amount of spent ammunition falling all round us was much more frightening than anything else. The tracer gave a display surpassing any of Brock's Benefits. Two enemy planes were seen to fall in flames, but the noise was so deafening that it was impossible to hear them or even hear bombs falling. Little damage was done and there was no direct hits; the only ships that suffered were the ones that had near misses and were thoroughly drenched by the spray thrown up. The landing had evidently caught the German Air Force as well as the Army by surprise, as it was not until the following night that attacks became heavy.

At first light all the craft were still milling about waiting for a chance to land their vehicles. The sea was still rough enough to make the craft more uncomfortable and to bring a lot of spray aboard. There did not seem to be any future in waiting for others in front to land and so our skipper prepared to make a run for the shore, with us feeling that anything would be better than staying aboard. With everyone on their vehicles and drivers holding their brakes, the craft speeded up and rushed the sandy shore. With luck we missed the many sandbanks and, passing with cheers the craft which were stuck and would have to wait for the high tide, we ran up well and stopped, leaving only about thirty yards of water to drive through with a maximum depth of 4 feet. It was all very different from what we expected. Whereas we had been prepared to land with "one up the spout" and with shells falling all around, our only real worry was to get our kit ashore dry. Now came the time when all our efforts with the waterproofing material were to be

finally tested. The ramp was lowered and the experts, testing the depth with sticks, ordered the first vehicle into the water. With cheers and facetious advice, the vehicle moved down the ramp at·a steep angle with everyone quite prepared for everything to disappear under the waves. But as the water was coming up to the driver's window the sand was reached and slowly the vehicle ploughed ashore, the crew gesticulating wildly. Encouraged, the other vehicles soon followed and everyone drove across the sand past other boats stranded by the high tide and past tanks stuck in soft patches and a few blown up by mines. Moving through a safe lane, we got onto a road and soon were in a field removing some of the waterproofing which had been so successful.

And so we had landed, relieved to be away from the uncomfortable and never-still craft, relieved that all was peaceful, and happy to hear again the cry "Brew up".' (From the Victory Number of the Eleventh Hussar Journal and published here by kind permission of Home Headquarters, The Royal Hussars.)

Top: An RASC vehicle belonging to the Divisional Supply Column leaves the ramp of a landing craft on its way to the land. Over 100 000 tons of stores were landed on the bridgehead in the first seven days.

Above: Into Battle. Cromwells of 4 CLY leaving the Normandy beaches – the great advance had started!

Caen, 1944. Probably the most devastated town in Normandy. Caen was pounded to rubble by continual air raids. Despite this treatment the citizens showed touching examples of gratitude for liberation and kept the graves of Allied soldiers fresh with flowers.

A Class 40 Bailey Pontoon Bridge across the River Seine at Les Andelys near Louviers constructed by 6 Army Troop Engineers Aug 29th-31st, 1944 – length 440 ft.

Welcome Monty! Graffiti on the walls of Malines, Belgium which the Division reached on September 11th from Ghent after 'an extremely pleasant march – grand reception everywhere and all vehicles finished laden with fruit and tomatoes'.

Villers Bocage – scene of one of the Division's toughest encounters in Europe.

North West Europe

North West Europe
Route taken by
Seventh Armoured Division
June 1944 - July 1945

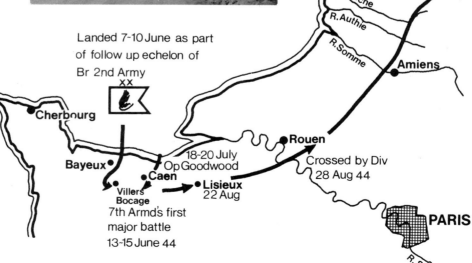

Holding the line-Static warfare 28 Sept 21 Oct 44

Rotterdam

Antwerp

Ghent   R.Scheldt

Wetteren

Dunkirk   Liberation of
Ghent 6 Sept

Calais

BRUSSE

Boulogne   Lille   Defence of t
Wetteren bri
5-6 S
R. Canche

R. Authie

R. Somme   Amiens

Landed 7-10 June as part
of follow up echelon of
Br 2nd Army
XX

Cherbourg

Rouen

Bayeux   Crossed by Div
18-20 July   28 Aug 44
Op Goodwood

Caen   Lisieux
Villers   22 Aug
Bocage
7th Armd's first
major battle
13-15 June 44

PARIS

R. Seine

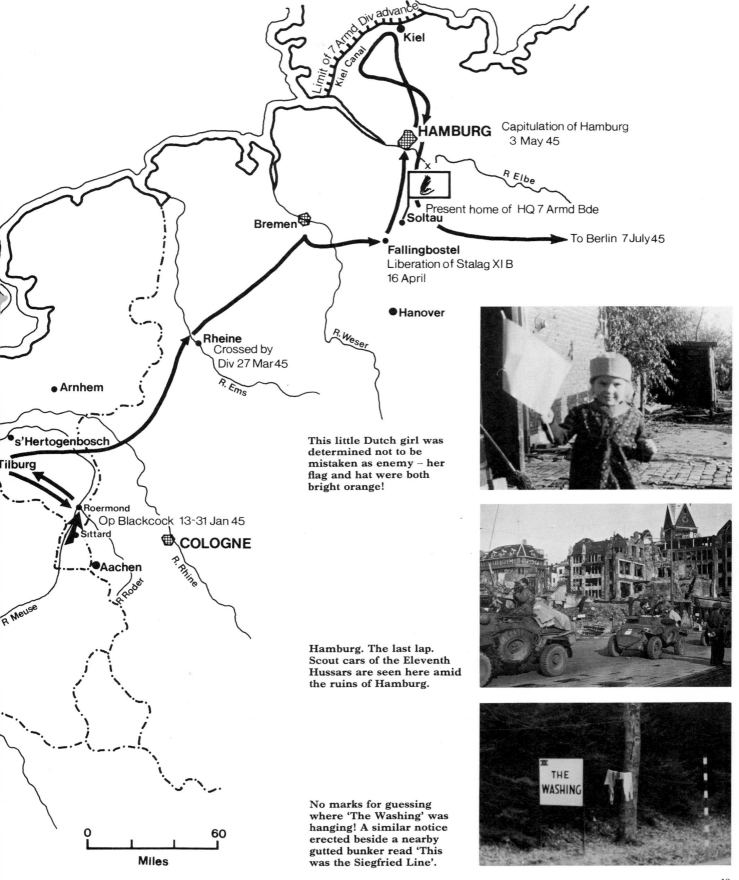

Limit of 7 Armd Div advance

Kiel

Kiel Canal

HAMBURG Capitulation of Hamburg
3 May 45

R Elbe

Present home of HQ 7 Armd Bde

Soltau

To Berlin 7 July 45

Bremen

Fallingbostel
Liberation of Stalag XI B
16 April

R. Weser

●**Hanover**

Rheine
Crossed by
Div 27 Mar 45

R. Ems

●**Arnhem**

■**s'Hertogenbosch**

Tilburg

●Roermond
Op Blackcock 13-31 Jan 45

Sittard

⌖**COLOGNE**

●**Aachen**

R Roder

R. Rhine

R Meuse

0 ────────── 60

Miles

This little Dutch girl was
determined not to be
mistaken as enemy – her
flag and hat were both
bright orange!

Hamburg. The last lap.
Scout cars of the Eleventh
Hussars are seen here amid
the ruins of Hamburg.

THE
WASHING

No marks for guessing
where 'The Washing' was
hanging! A similar notice
erected beside a nearby
gutted bunker read 'This
was the Siegfried Line'.

59

Into the Bocage

Radio Bulletin
NOT FOR PUBLICATION, BROAD-
CAST IN OVERSEAS BULLETINS OR
USE ON CLUB TAPES BEFORE 23.30
DBST ON THURSDAY JULY 13TH, 1944
(I.E. FOR FRIDAY JULY 14TH MORN-
ING PAPERS). NOT TO BE BROAD-
CAST IN THE MIDNIGHT NEWS OF
JULY 13TH/14TH. THIS EMBARGO
SHOULD BE RESPECTED OVERSEAS
BY PREFACING ANY MESSAGES FILED
WITH THE EMBARGO.

7TH ARMOURED DIVISION TO JUNE 17TH 1944

'The 7th Armoured Division was among the vanguard of the British armour to be fighting in Normandy. By June 9th, elements of the Division were already concentrated at Caugy, and by the following day the formation was occupying positions in the Mendaye area.

From that time onwards the formation's story was one of sustained and bitter fighting in which it did superb service by breaking many counter-attacks and capturing positions held by powerful enemy forces. On June 11th it was in action in the Tilly area and here for several days it took part in mopping up German troops, advancing towards Hottot against stern reaction and, later, holding a line in the face of violent enemy counter-attacks.

By June 14th, the Division had established strongpoints in several villages among the low hills to the west of Villers Bocage, and here during the next few days, it repelled several enemy assaults taking a heavy toll of the German armour. On June 17th, in particular, the famous "Desert Rats" gained a remarkable success in destroying large forces of the enemy in a fierce action at Bricques-sard'.

The Bocage

The brief radio bulletin above tells little of the fierce action fought at Villers Bocage in which the Division really experienced for the first time the difficulties of fighting in the dense bocage countryside with its high hedges, sunken roads, thick standing crops and orchards, where the normal battle range was likely to be under 300 yards and camouflage and concealment were all important. They also discovered the unpleasant fact that their Shermans and Cromwells were usually no match for the opposing Tigers and Panthers, being outgunned and under-armoured. Villers Bocage was therefore no great victory, but the Desert Rats fought

The Division advancing southwards into the Bocage.

Top: Tank battle in Villers Bocage. A British tank (left) engaging a German Tiger muzzle to muzzle through the corner of a house. (Reproduced by kind permission of the Illustrated London News).

Above: Advancing through the Bocage.

tenaciously and with great courage throughout, suffering considerable casualties.

The Outline Plan
The main aim of the British 2nd Army at that time was to capture Caen and a pincer movement was launched with 51st Highland Division to the east of the town, and 50th Division and 7th Armoured Division to the west. Neither arm of the pincer was parparticularly successful and on June 11th the operation was temporarily halted, the German Panzer Lehr Division proving too tough a nut to crack.

Meanwhile, however, the Americans had

been able to push inland some 20 miles from Omaha beach, forming a deep salient around Caumont. It was therefore decided that 7th Armoured would wheel behind 50th Division, strike south so that it was advancing parallel with the Americans around Caumont, and then turn due east again to take first Villers Bocage and then Caen from the flank. Unfortunately for the Desert Rats their vanguard, composed of the 4th County of London Yeomanry, 'A' Company 1st Rifle Brigade and 'B' Battery 5th Royal Horse Artillery, ran into 501 Waffen SS Heavy Tank Battalion shortly after leaving Villers Bocage on the road to Caen. This battalion was equipped with Tiger and Panther tanks which were occupying good fire positions in the close bocage countryside and wrought havoc amongst the British armour. The story of this engagement is told by Major Christopher Milner, MC, who was at that time second in command of 'A' Company, 1RB.

Christopher Milner
'As we passed through the small town of Villers Bocage we were greeted with interest rather than enthusiasm by the small groups of people standing about: "Les pompiers", (the fire brigade) I recollect, being much in evidence in one area; they might have warned of trouble if one had had time to stop, but I was on my way in my half track

Left: Carriers of the Queens take to a cornfield to bypass enemy opposition.

Below: Jerry shells here. Fine weather brought clouds of dust along the unmetalled roads, and the dust in its turn brought German shells – hence this common roadside sign to limit vehicle speeds.

Bottom: A Sherman Firefly. The 17-pounder of the Firefly was one of the few tank guns capable of dealing with German Tigers and Panthers. This one belonged to 4 CLY.

from the rear to the front of the company, picking up the platoon commanders and the mortar sergeant en route, in response to an urgent 'O' group summons from my company commander, James Wright. He in turn had just been briefed by Arthur, Viscount Cranley, commanding 4 CLY, at Point 210, the top of the low hill about 1½ miles east of the town – and our objective.

We were motoring rapidly along the straight road, past the dismounted riflemen and their evenly spaced half-tracks, but not past the scout platoon because Alan Mather's carriers had been shipped in a different vessel and they had not yet caught up with us. As this officer proved subsequently before he was killed, he was a particularly able and resourceful carrier commander and the outcome of the battle might have been very different if the force commander had had the benefit of information from this very experienced reconnaissance platoon to draw upon, in addition to that received from the tired and over-stretched armoured car squadron. As we shall see, had they been available to protect the southern flank of the regimental group as it swung from south to east, not only might the German tanks have been rumbled much earlier (since the parallel track which the enemy followed would have provided even better cover for the low-slung carriers) but one can even speculate upon a

fantastically different outcome of the Normandy battle if only this break-through had been successful enough to enable the Queen's Brigade to follow through the gap and dig in behind the German lines on this exceedingly important feature.

Things would also have been different had the platoon commanders been with their men – or even at a pinch, if I had been available at the rear of the company to rally them – either forward on to point 210 (the German tanks would have been terribly vulnerable to intelligent soldiers behind those thickly-banked bocage hedges, as our own tank commanders would readily testify) or back into the town, where their presence could have made all the difference to the CLY, who were trapped in the narrow streets without the riflemen stirrup-hangers who had been trained to work with them in just such conditions. Anyway, none of these things happened; instead, when my truck had just

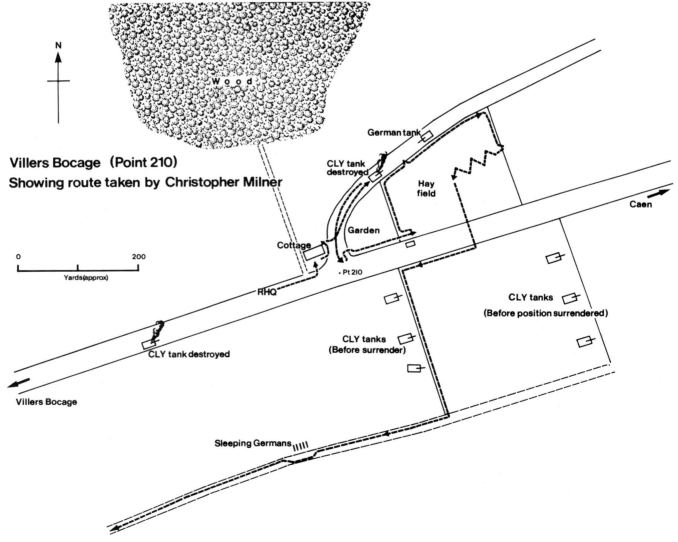

Villers Bocage (Point 210)
Showing route taken by Christopher Milner

Far left, top: Villers Bocage
in ruins after the battle.

Above: A Panther burns.

passed the rearmost CLY tank (which was
facing forward, suspecting nothing) at the
foot of the rise, the tank was hit and burst into
flames. As we passed the next one (it had a
high turret and was a 17 pounder) perhaps a
100 yards further on, it swung round and
began to engage whatever had shot-up its
neighbour from the south. A minute later we
dismounted by the cottage at the lane
junction which lies at point 210, to join a
shaken 'O' group in circumstances which had
changed utterly since it had been called.

There followed a period of physical in-
activity on point 210, whilst the enemy
attended first of all to the three motor
platoons by cutting the road behind us and
then trundling back towards Villers Bocage,
shooting up vehicles and riflemen section by
section, with only the company's two 6
pounder anti-tank guns able to offer even a
measure of resistance; which, I learned afterwards, they did with considerable bravery
but with little effect upon the German
Tigers and Panthers which joined battle with
the two CLY squadrons in the town.

The force on point 210 consisted, then, of
Colonel Cranley and his Tac HQ, one
depleted squadron of Cromwells, a gunner
OP officer, OC 'A' Company (James Wright)
and all his officers (except the one commanding the leading platoon, who had run back to
his men and was, I think, killed with them),
the mortar section and one section only of
riflemen. The CLY tanks had fanned out a
little, but apart from intermittent harassment

by shellfire, the Germans left us to our own
devices whilst they dealt with the main body
of the regimental group. We were stonked at
intervals during the morning and suffered
one particular casualty which grieved us very
much – a young officer who had only just
joined and as I recall it, one whose mother
later could never really accept that he had no
chance to live because he was captured still
alive and for months afterwards she wrote the
most tragic letters to me, trying to believe
that he had not died. Anyway, the infantry
section I put on the southern side, covering
what I discovered afterwards was the track
parallel to the main road along which the
German tanks had been shadowing us, though
no more appeared on our particular high
point until a little later. I set myself to cover
the lane running east north east from point
210 and the mortar sergeant covered the track
leading into and out of the wood directly to
our north. I was behind a small cottage. It was
along this track that a peasant woman walked
up to us, was detained as a possible spy, but
after an hour or so she slipped away. Was she
a spy?

Not long after, a CLY tank, edging forward around the bend along my lane, was hit
and the wounded crew baled out having
suffered the driver killed. They seemed to be
pinned down so I crawled along the road and
helped them to get back to the comparative
safety of the cottage. I then lay on watch
again, armed with a sten gun, my pistol and,
I half remember, a German Luger without

Normandy Obstacles.
Taking every advantage of
the natural defensive
features of the Normandy
countryside, the Germans
make dugouts in hedgerows,
build concrete strong points
for mortar crews in
orchards, use farm workers
as decoys and employ
many other tricks in an
attempt to trap Allied troops
and armour or to hide from
our observers their strengths
and dispositions.
(Reproduced by kind
permission of the Illustrated
London News).

any ammunition. Suddenly there was a rumble of tanks from the east and as I darted round to the front of the cottage I was astonished to find that the tank shooting seemed to have ended and that some officers in black berets were standing about talking to one or two of our officers in the middle of the main road. Since there had been no shooting and everyone seemed very friendly I took them to be members of the Royal Tank Regiment and stepped out to join in the conversation, only to be frozen in my tracks when I realised that they were German tank crews.

I immediately turned and didn't run back where I'd come from but ducked into a little garden to the left and ran up inside the hedge in the direction of the enemy, not of our own people in Villers Bocage. I went through a little gate beyond the garden still just inside the hedge with one of the German officers running along the road parallel to me shouting "Englishman surrender! Englishman surrender!" Fortunately he stopped after about fifty yards and talked to another officer who'd just arrived from the German side in a Volkswagen and at this stage I decided that it was about time I died a hero's death and so I stood up and levelled my sten gun at the two of them, at pretty well point blank range over the top of the hedge, took careful aim and pressed the trigger. But of

course, like so many sten guns, it decided not to work and just had the effect of sobering me up! I concluded that perhaps it wasn't a good thing after all to draw attention to myself in this way; so I turned left up the inside of a hedge, which was actually running due north, and crept quietly along until to my horror I saw a German boot sticking out of it; I thought my number was up. However, creeping up very carefully and slowly I was relieved but disconcerted to find that the leg in the boot belonged to a dead German soldier.

Keeping low down under the lee of the hedge (which like most in the Bocage was on top of a three foot high bank) I turned right, round the northern edge of this little hayfield, found a gap and decided that the best thing to do was to make a break for it, since I could memorise the map of the district. If I could cut across this lane (which was the same one that I had been guarding previously) I could then make my way back to our own lines through the large wood which lay to the north. I gingerly let myself down the bank on the other side feet first and peeked to my right, only to find that I was about twenty yards from the muzzle of a German tank's gun which, had I thought a bit more care-carefully, would have been the one which knocked out the Cromwell whose crew I had helped a little earlier. Very fortunately (and

The GOC, Major General Verney, in his scout car near Lille.

not for the last time that day) nobody seemed to notice me, so I pulled myself back up the bank, through the hedge, and crouching down, thought again. I had now been on three sides of the hayfield and it only left the fourth side. I had a brain-wave that perhaps the best thing to do was to climb up into one of the trees which grew out of the bank and make myself inconspicuous there until darkness fell and perhaps I could then get out and return to our lines.

So I crawled, by this time on my belly, round the outside of the field and found a suitable place to lever myself up to the bank top and look through the bottom of the hedge to see what was happening the other side, that is to say in the direction of the German lines – only to find that I was frustrated yet again, because in the middle of that field there had just arrived a German troop of guns, which was busily digging itself in and would obviously make my life uncomfortable from the noise and the blasts, or might take it upon itself to notice me and that would be that.

All this time there had been rumblings and shouts along the main road, but for some extraordinary reason, although the hedge on the main road side was not very high, no one seemed to look into my field. Anyway, it seemed the only thing to do was to somehow stay there and remain inconspicuous, so I

gradually wormed my way along a zig-zag course, in order that someone passing by the end of my track in the hay (which wasn't very high – about one foot six) wouldn't be able to look along my little belly track and see where I was. I stopped in about the middle of the hayfield and lay still to think things over. By this time, I suppose, it must have been early afternoon and I started wondering what had happened to everybody else.

Not very surprisingly I wasn't the only person thinking along these lines, because I hadn't been in this position very long when there was a wizz and an explosion and a smoke shell landed quite near me, followed by another one and then a whole smoke screen laid itself across the middle of my little field, probably some excellent RHA gunners who were obviously doing their best, although rather too late, to give us some protection behind which we could withdraw. Anyway the shells landed and it was difficult not to cough an awful lot, they gradually gave up and all was peaceful. It was a nice fine afternoon, the sun was shining and I suppose I went to sleep for a bit. The only snag was that I was incredibly hungry and not a little thirsty, because I don't remember if I had a water bottle; if I had, there was precious little in it. At any rate I survived this tedious afternoon and evening and at last it began to get dark and I started to crawl slowly towards the main road again, that is to say towards the south side of the field. My plan was now to wait until all was clear, dash across the main road, over the intervening field to the parallel track (that is to say the Panther tanks' track) and, once again remembering the map, turn back in a westerly direction towards Villers Bocage and try to take a course which would bring me round the south side of the town instead of the north – or into the town itself if that was where our own troops were.

At last, perhaps around midnight, when the Germans decided that they might as well have a rest, there was a lull with no vehicles passing and fortunately it was dark without, as far as I can remember, much in the way of a moon. So I was able to sprint across the road, dive into the hedge on the far side and creep along the inside of the hedge until I hit the track. No one seemed to have spotted me or took any notice so I stood up and walked gingerly along the grass track, back towards the town, which was perhaps a mile and a half away. Suddenly I heard a very odd noise, surprisingly like several people snoring and in point of fact I was quite right, it was snoring and it came from a section of German soldiers who had dug a broad shallow trench, wrapped themselves in their blankets and, having piled their arms beside the trench, were all sound asleep. I had no idea where their sentry was but I was lucky because I didn't spot the piled arms until I was perhaps twenty five yards away. Anyway, I crept past and after a while found myself coming into a farm-yard. I don't think that even a dog barked, if it did it didn't take much notice of me and the great thing was that I found a trough full of drinkable water and I remember taking off my beret (which had been rendered pretty well waterproof by the combination of grease and sweat in my hair over a year or two) and it held water remarkably well. I had an extremely good drink.

It was still uncanny to find no one about. However, I pressed on and came to the railway sidings on the south side of the town, across which I had to go in order to reach the far side and take the road back the way we had come early the previous morning. Then another astonishing thing occurred, because a number of shells started to fall on the British side of the town, followed not long afterwards by a number of shells on the German side of the town, yet so far as I could tell neither army had any troops there by way of targets. After a while things calmed down and I continued on my way unmolested, across the railway tracks and would certainly have been spotted immediately if there had been anybody about, but there didn't seem to be any civilians around either. At last I reached the western side of the town and I remember walking judiciously along the side of the road until I came to some tank tracks leading into a field. So I turned into it, not quite knowing whether they were our tracks or those of the enemy and tried to work out which they were without coming to any clear decision. At any rate there were no tanks or vehicles around, so I went back on to the road and continued walking along the south side where at this point there seemed to be a fairly high bank which provided a certain amount of shadow, because I had a feeling that there was a moon getting up by now.

Below: Aunay-sur-Odon from the south.

Above: Cromwells of the Skins being prepared for battle.

Suddenly (as they say in the books) I froze to the ground because I was challenged, and to this day I can't be sure whether it was a German or a British soldier, because the words if you drop an "H" are absolutely identical if you want someone to stop – "alt"! After a second call I still wasn't sure, so I scrambled as fast as I could up the bank, through a fence, dashed down the side of a hedge and was just in time to fling myself into it as a Verey light went up and obviously the soldier had called one of his mates and they were starting to investigate where I was. Having lain in this spot for a little while and having decided that they were going back to

their sentry post, I went on back towards our lines, aiming to get on to the main road at a suitable distance along it – alternatively lying up for a quarter of an hour and then creeping along and listening very carefully in case I heard any sounds. Then, as dawn was really starting to break, I heard some noises in a farm house and so gave it a wide circuit and eventually came on to the blessed road, by which time it was daylight. Still no one saw me apparently, or challenged me and, rounding a bend, at last I saw what I had been looking for and that was part of our own brigade and its vehicles. I remember that I turned off down a side track and the next thing I found that I was amongst a regimental cook-house and was cadging a large billy-can full of bacon, plus a mug of tea.

So that was my battle of Villers Bocage, not very glorious I'm afraid and yet of any twenty-four hours in my life I can think of none which I can recall so clearly as I can those hours, which photographed themselves in my mind so that now, telling the story God knows thirty years later, I can see every yard of the route which I followed and every episode as clearly as if it had happened last year'.

The Enemy
The Tiger tank which caused the initial carnage was commanded by Ober Sturmfuhrer SS Michel Wittman, who knocked out 25 vehicles in that one engagement to add

to his already incredible tally of 119 Soviet tanks destroyed during his service on the Russian front! It was an exploit which 'almost made a legend of the man who held up an entire armoured division and contributed not insignificantly to the events which followed' Wittman was killed shortly after this engagement. (Profile *AFV Weapons Book No 48* by P. Chamberlain and C. Ellis.)

The 'Skins' join the Division
'Fare thee well Inniskilling! Fare thee well for a while
To all your fair waters and every green isle!
And when the war is over we'll return again soon
And they'll all welcome home the Inniskilling Dragoon'.
(Last verse of 'The Inniskilling Dragoon').

On July 29th the 4th County of London Yeomanry were transferred to 4th Armoured Brigade to amalgamate with their sister regiment the 3rd CLY, because there were no longer enough reinforcements to keep both Regiments up to strength. 4th CLY had been with the Division since 1942 so it was a sad parting. Their place was taken by the 5th Royal Inniskilling Dragoon Guards newly arrived from England. They were soon to be in action as Operation 'Bluecoat' was about to begin. The initial aim of the British 2nd Army was to capture Mont Pincon, south of Aunay-sur-Odon, so within two days of joining the Division the 'Skins'

were in battle for the first time since Dunkirk. As their Regimental history explains they felt very much the new boys:

'The column of new tanks bearing the freshly painted divisional and brigade signs, the desert rat and the stag's head, made their way into harbour about Juaye Mendaye, some four miles to the south of Bayeux, to take over from the Sharpshooters. "What mob are you?" inquired a bearded and grimy visage looking over the top of a scarred and battered turret, "Never 'eard of yer!" remarked the face after explanations had been offered, and with that devastating comment it sank back into the dark and oily depths. In this distinguished company, where highly coloured corduroy trousers, brilliant pullovers and gaudy scarves were de rigeur – where, it was rumoured, the sand of the desert still lurked in shoes and ears – the 5th Royal Inniskilling Dragoon Guards still had their spurs to win'. (The 5th Royal Inniskilling Dragoon Guards, by Maj Gen R. Evans, CB, MC.)

A Troop Leader's View
What was it like to be a troop leader in that newly joined regiment? Brigadier Henry Woods, MBE, MC, who was then a young troop leader in 'C' Squadron, recalls his first action:

'After the breakout from the Normandy beaches 7th Armoured Division advanced almost due north from the area of St Pierre-sur-Dives (SW of Caen). The movement began on August 16th 1944, and the divisional axis of advance was developed through Livarot, Lisieux and Montfort, being directed towards the lower reaches of the Seine. During the night 26th/27th 5 Innis DG harboured in the area of Bonneville Appetot, and during the morning of the 27th, C Squadron attempted to advance north on Bonneville in thickish country very like the bocage of the beach head fighting. Tiny fields and orchards, thick hedgerows and small copses made the country very small, and in many of the fields were fine herds of cattle. Alive, they suggested rich milk, fine butter and Camembert cheese as a welcome addition to compo rations. Dead, the sickening stench from their bloated bodies permeated everything even the tea one drank and the food one ate. To all who fought in Normandy, the smell of death lives longest in the memory.

Between noon and 2 pm B Squadron passed through C and advanced into the village of Bonneville Appetot and out on two routes leading north and north west. About a mile out on the northern route 3 Tp, B Sqn ran into trouble. Picture them moving forward across a large open common, with a long wood on the right and some small fields and farm buildings on the left, beneath a bright summer sky. The trees, hedgerows and grass are lush in the late summer, and looking north the country slopes gently downwards in a series of wooded ridges. Beyond one of these – in fact about six miles away, the River Seine flows between Rouen and Le Havre. As the leading tank rumbles to the corner of the hedgerow near the farm house – the driver's next bound – the white dust streams away from the tracks and seems to float momentarily before dispersing on the wind. Suddenly, there is a sharp crack like a large nutcracker smashing an enormous walnut. At the same moment the leading tank lurches, a bright flash winks on the right front of the turret. With gathering speed the tank jinks off the road, crashes through the hedgerow to the left and then right to the corner of the orchard by the farm.

On the radio the set phrases of a SITREP uttered in staccato tones reveal the urgent crisis of the moment. Though the leading tank has been hit on the corner of the turret which is jammed, the crew are unhurt. The rest of the troop have also moved rapidly to

B Squadron of the Skins forming up for an attack near Aunay-sur-Odon.

71

fire positions in the same area. Tank commanders are busy searching the area whence the fire came, but at this stage of the war, the enemy are still highly skilled in the tactical siting and camouflage of their fearsome 88mm anti-tank guns, and in the hot summer afternoon, there is no indication of exactly where the gun which fired is or where its inevitable companions might be. A lull descends temporarily while the troop and squadron leaders wrestle with the problem of whether to risk another tank brewed up by moving into the open and drawing fire. The CO is involved and decides that the risk is too much without fire support and covering fire. 2 Lt Bradfield and his crews sit watching.

Meanwhile 1st Tp C Sqn, which I commanded was still just south of the village. Since noon, we have had a hasty sandwich of bully beef and a brew of tea, and I have found time to purchase a chicken, cheese, fresh milk and butter from a small farm. These are now stowed in the left-hand bin above the tracks of my tank. Like soldiers throughout the ages, stowage diagrams and instructions, whether covering personal or vehicle equipment, are more honoured in the breach than the observance, and much of the kit which should be in that bin is festooned around the rear of the turret. Being on a squadron net, we have heard only very garbled and summary reports of what has occurred to B Sqn. But the pause now ends and as C Sqn Leader, Major Ward-Harrison speeds back from the CO's Tac HQ, we troop leaders are summoned over the radio to an 'O' Group. Clutching map-boards,

chinagraph pencils and notebooks we double across to the Sqn Leader's scout car. The gist of the orders for me is that 1st Tp is to reinforce B Sqn at once, and to move forward and join up with 3 Tp B Sqn, at which stage I will come under command. A quick glance at the small scale maps (all we have) does not give me the truth about the lie of the land north of the village, and with hindsight I did not then realise than 3 Tp B Sqn was well over the crest and on a forward slope. Urged on by an angry demand from Sqn HQ to know why I am not on the move, I give very hasty orders to my crew commanders, shout "mount" and 1st Tp are soon rolling in column through the village. As we clear the houses I order the troop to deploy "two up", which means two Cromwells supported in the second rank by one Cromwell and the Sherman 17 pdr Firefly. My tank is left forward, and we are almost shaken out into formation as we cross the crest.

There is a violent flash on the front of the right forward Tp Cpl's tank, and it stops. Within seconds it is clearly "brewed up", as smoke wraiths trickle from the engine and the turret. The crew pop out like champagne corks, seeming to flow down the front and sides to the ground as though diving feet first. We all realise our exposed position, but luckily I am able to halt the rear two tanks so that they are hull-down on the crest. I switch onto the inter-comm and order the driver to wheel hard left and get back behind the crest, jinking as we go. We are almost back to the crest, when suddenly there is a jarring thud,

the driver reports that all his controls have gone and I look down to see smoke wisping through the engine covers. We are also "brewed up", and there is nothing for it but to bail out. As I leap from the turret which is still traversed over the rear, my beret comes off, but I catch it on my little finger before I reach the ground. My Tp Cpl's crew are under cover behind a small bank beside the road, atop of which is a wayside wooden Calvary and we double across to join them. As we go the crackling hiss of machine gun bullets spurs us on. Panting, we fling ourselves down behind the tank, and for a few seconds there is peace, shattered by first of all my Tp Cpl's tank and then my own roaring into flames. No one has yet spotted where the enemy guns are, but at least except for two minor wounds, we are all alive.

Apart from my rage at losing two tanks in less than a minute, all those excellent farm supplies have gone west, and the chicken is burnt beyond recall. Now it is time for more action, and I evict my troop sergeant from his tank, and he takes the dismounted crews back into the village to Sqn HQ. The CO decides not to try to advance due north by the obviously well-covered approach, but to develop a thrust on the other route and out-flank this opposition. The sun is well down in the west by the time that the opposition has withdrawn and the Regiment finally reaches Bonneville. At that stage our advance to the lower Seine finished, and 7th Armoured Division was pulled out to rejoin 12 Corps for the great swan up to Belgium. We never did taste that chicken!'

Belgium ~ 'You are Quite Welcome'

General Verney, GOC 7th Armoured Division, arriving in Ghent in a Staghound Armoured Car, September 8th, 1944.

Monty gives his orders. Gen Verney GOC, Seventh Armoured Division is on the right of the picture.

where. What is equally heart-warming is the way in which this friendship has stood the test of time and is still as strong today as it was over thirty years ago.

Full Speed for Ghent! The Ghent Force
At mid-day on September 4th, 1944, General Verney, GOC 7th Armoured Division, warned a special force to prepare for what he hoped would be 'the last long gallop for Ghent'. The size of the force to be sent had to be worked out very carefully as the petrol used by the Division had been averaging over 70 000 gallons a day – that was seventy lorry loads. So it was out of the question to move more than a composite brigade on that final seventy mile dash. The Ghent Force, as it was called, was commanded by a reduced Main Divisional HQ and comprised the 11th Hussars, Main HQ 22nd Armoured Brigade, 5th RHA, 5th Innis DG, 5th RTR, 1/6th Queens and 'A' Company 1st RB. Extra petrol lorries from 8th Hussars, 1st RTR and the Rifle Brigade accompanied the force. The remainder of the Division stayed in their positions around Bethune and did their best to keep the Centre Line open.

The Force Advances
That afternoon the Cherry Pickers led the force out, their initial objective being to secure a crossing over the river at Audenarde, scene of Marlborough's famous battle. Whilst the force was advancing members of the Belgian resistance were themselves in action. One of these resistance fighters, 'From' Fromont, takes up the story:

'Tanks on the way to Ghent from Audenarde, September 4th, 1944 at 1600 hours. We of the Belgian resistance had had some days of hard work before then rounding up pro-German civilians and taking them to a safe place called "The Pinte" where they could be protected from the rest of the population and also to stop them from giving information to the Germans about Allied troop movements, as it soon became well known to the civilian population that the British were on their way.

I return for a moment to the day before – September 3rd at about 1900 hours – when a large German patrol consisting of one officer, two sergeants and about 60 troopers, all on bicycles and heavily armed with automatic weapons and hand grenades, passed through St Denis-Westrem on the main road from Ghent to Courtai. We, the resistance men,

An Even Greater Welcome
The wonderful welcome which the British troops had received in France was even more enthusiastic when they crossed the frontier into Belgium. As the War Diary of the 3rd Regiment, Royal Horse Artillery commented: 'Even more flowers, larger and better fruit – an even greater welcome'. There were flags everywhere, on the churches, on the houses and many banners hung across the roads with such inscriptions as 'Vive les Anglais!' Welcome!', 'Well Done!' and even one which must have been the understatement of the war, reading 'You are quite welcome'! I have chosen two incidents from this period of the advance, first the liberation of the old city of Ghent by tanks of A Squadron, 5th Royal Tank Regiment and second, the defence of the bridge at Wetteren over the River Schelde, by 4th Field Squadron, Royal Engineers. Both have in common the tremendous friendship shown to the Desert Rats by Belgian civilians every-

only had revolvers and we were only seven in all, but we had a very fast car. The driver, a resistance officer, a sergeant of the Belgian Army and myself, followed the Germans at a safe distance. After a while they turned back, so we quickly had to leave the main road and take a side track into Lathem–St Martin, where to our great surprise we saw a company of about three hundred Germans, all armed, taking a rest in a field. No need to say that we passed them at full speed! We returned to St Denis–Westrem that night and had to send many civilians home, they were still standing along the road carrying flowers and fruit for the incoming Allied forces!

The next day we took some German soldiers prisoner as well as more pro-German civilians and moved all of them to "The Pinte". At about 1300 hours I went to take a rest in the house of a friend – Madame de Volqelaire. Her first husband had died during the 1914-1918 War and her second husband died in 1940 in action; he was a major in the Belgian Army. She herself, although not a full time member of the Resistance, helped us whenever she could. She woke me up at about 1600 hours telling me the best news I had ever received, the news that we had been waiting for all of those last four years – "The English are here!" I ran out of the villa, down the lane, onto the main road, and there they were! Tanks were taking up positions to defend the cross roads – The Pinte – St Denis – Westrem. I remember very well that there were only seven tanks, later I got to know that this was all that was left of "A" Squadron, 5th Royal Tank Regiment, the rest being out of action along the road from Audenarde.

The first officer I spoke to – my English was all right since my late mother was a Scot and we always spoke English at home – was Lt Roy Dixon, now Director of British Army Aviation. I offered my services, he took me down to a Cromwell tank with a short gun-barrel and introduced me to Captain Stuart Jones. All the men were dirty and very tired. Captain Jones accepted my services, but I felt he did not trust me! Quite right too, I would not have done so in his place, but I thought "Time will tell".

September 5th. Our work as resistance men went on as before. The civil population from Ghent about 5 miles away came down to greet the liberators! That afternoon a motorised German 88 came from Courtai. One of the tank commanders, Lt Zoeftig, tried to fire at it, but as civilians were running about

The Ghent Citation. **Presented to the 5th Royal Tank Regiment in honour of their being the first Regiment to enter Ghent.**

all over the place he could not do so without harming them. After a while the 88 came back along another road and later its crew destroyed it and escaped.

On the morning of September 6th a German railway gun fired one shell which struck a pole next to the tank belonging to the Squadron Sergeant Major of "A" Squadron who was very badly hurt and died that same afternoon. Lt Zoeftig, having been told that 300 German troops were camped at Lathem–St Martin got permission to go and get them – but only with one tank. I went with him and Lt Zoeftig arranged with a Belgian Major named Ham, for the capitulation of these Germans. Their small arms went to the Resistance and the Germans were marched down the road to St Denis–Westrem, parked in a field and later were marched to the nearby village of Nazareth. The Resistance patrolled the road to Ghent, but no Germans were to be seen. Captain Stuart Jones risked his own tank and a Humber

The Ghent Medallion, presented to the Division, now on show in the RAC Tank Museum, Bovington Camp, Dorset.

Scout car to go into Ghent. I went with him on the tank, he riding on the "Dingo" driven by Sergeant Harry Hampton. We went as far as the Town Hall where he drank champagne with the town officials, whilst we stayed outside trying to keep the people away. After that we returned to the cross-roads at St Denis–Westrem. We took some more prisoners and that same day the seven tanks of "A" Squadron, all went into Ghent to take up positions at St Pieters station and other important places on the north side of the city. The day after, September 7th, the tanks went up to the industrial area named "Rabot". There Captain Butler was badly wounded and died later in a Military Hospital at Eeklo and was buried at the Canadian Cemetery in Odeqem and still rests there. In that industrial area the 51st Highland Division joined in to fight the Germans.

Many people think that it was the Poles who liberated Ghent, but the real liberator was Captain Stuart Jones with his "Dingo" and his one tank'.

Recollection of the Liberation
One of the seven tank commanders, Lt Ted Zoeftig also recalls the first moments of liberation:

'My own special recollections – for what they are worth – concern that time as we came towards the centre of the town. People were lining the streets in thickening numbers. Flowers were beginning to heap up over our

blanket rolls and over the engine plates, the lap-gunner's gun and against the turret. But the stream of people swished forward like a stream of silver sound which flowed and surged into the square, behind us and around us. It surged and swirled with a single continuous sound of happiness and joy, a chorus of exhultation which focussed on us, around us and now so it seemed, above us. The bells were ringing. In our sorry clothing, oil stained and petrol washed; tank track guards dented and holed, tow ropes hanging loose, scarecrow replicas of regimental dress, we tried desperately to be "The Liberators". We kept our positions, we remained alert for an unlikely sniper, the gunner at his gun, the driver cautiously keeping the tank moving, the wireless operator on watch and the troop leader vigilant. But this swelling silver sound was music. This must indeed have been the music that returning victorious legions of Rome had heard. A momentary approbation to forget, for a space, our soldiers' role. Now all the simple plain young men crewing the tank were enveloped – embraced – possessed, by the God-sent thanks. The tracks squeaked and stopped rolling. The surges of golden faces and hands swept up to us, and, for a moment, over us. Then for a short while the spirit of this brooding antique town claimed the five of us. Bedecked like natives of Hawaii, gifts were thrown, kisses given, treasured bottles of liqueurs, kept from the dark days of 1940 for just this longed for moment, were thrust home into our hands. Small wonder that none who experienced it

can forget or escape one single facet of that crystallised moment of glory'.

The Defence of the Wetteren Bridge, Belgium
(September 5-6, 1944)

Fighting Soldiers First

In any phase of war the Royal Engineers are worth their weight in gold, because there are always far too many jobs to be done which call for the sappers' special know-how and expertise. Therefore, it is unusual for them to be required to fight as infantry soldiers. They are of course trained for this task first and foremost and have on numerous occasions proved their prowess. The defence of the important bridge at Wetteren, over the River Schelde, was one such occasion.

The Battle in Outline

Wetteren lies to the east of Ghent and the bridge there had been partly damaged by a German demolition party. 4th Field Squadron, Royal Engineers, was given the dual task of repairing the bridge and of defending it. They started work, but hardly had they begun, when they were attacked by a reinforced company of SS troops, supported by heavy mortars and anti-tank guns. A fierce fight ensued which lasted all night and most of the next day. Tanks of C Squadron, 5th Royal Inniskilling Dragoon Guards finally arrived on the scene to tip the scales, but in the meantime the sappers had fought magnificently, defending the bridge against repeated enemy attacks. This is the story of their battle.

September 5th, 1944

A Squadron 5DG reached Wetteren at about midday on the 5th and at once approached the bridge. It was a three span affair on timber piles, the centre span being a lifting span, pivoting at the near bank with the aid of a counter weight. This span was found to be raised and the enemy were evidently intending to demolish the bridge, indeed, they had already made two unsuccessful attempts.

Major Fitzgerald, DSO, the OC of 4th Field Squadron, was with the tanks and quickly realised that the bridge must be lowered so that our infantry could get across and clear the enemy from the far bank. So, whilst the tanks put down covering fire, he dashed across the open square, together with some local civilians and climbed on to the raised portion of the bridge – their combined weight caused the span to drop into place. This bold move was carried out under the very noses of the enemy who were taken completely by surprise. Sappers then rushed forward and put some timber on to the damaged superstructure of the bridge, which allowed the infantry to cross and to clear the immediate area around the bridge taking a good many prisoners. The sappers then repaired the bridge sufficiently so as to allow the tanks and some armoured cars of the Eleventh Hussars to cross and to carry on with the advance.

The commander of 22nd Armoured Brigade then decided that, because of a drastic shortage of infantry, the sappers

Lt Ted Zoeftig's tank with German officer prisoners sitting on the back. It led the column of some 300 German soldiers whom he captured at Lathem St Martin.

General Verney arriving at the Ghent Town Hall, September 8th, 1944.

would have to defend the bridge as well as reinforcing it sufficiently so that it would take all the remaining Divisional traffic. Major Fitzgerald wirelessed back for his squadron and they motored up to Wetteren. Later, at his Orders group, he detailed a party to repair the bridge and then decided to take his troop leaders out on a recce to look for suitable defensive positions – it was now about 1600 hours.

Civilians Report 'Enemy!'
Civilians began to report that masses of German troops were approaching Wetteren from all directions, so Major Fitzgerald sent out recce parties down the various approach roads to the town. Sergeant Eric Morrall, MM, BEM, was in command of one of those recce patrols and now takes up the story:
'Once the centre span of the bridge had been lowered into position by Major Fitzgerald with the assistance of some brave local civilians, my troop, 1 Troop, under the command of Lt Jim Turpin (better known as "Dick") was called forward to defend the bridge.

I was first ordered by Lt Turpin, to recce the main road running north east from Wetteren and parallel with the river, where it had been reported by the local inhabitants that an enemy patrol was approaching the town. After about a mile or so we sighted the enemy by the river bank, heading in our direction. Small arms fire was exchanged and they withdrew, with the loss I believe of one killed. Later I was re-called by Lt Turpin, to the bridge where our Troop were digging in.

That evening all was quiet and everyone apart from the usual lookouts and guards were getting a little shut-eye. I was with Dicky Turpin in our troop headquarters in an old brickworks, bedding down between piles of bricks and chimney pots. Suddenly, during the night, small arms fire opened up and shortly afterwards two wounded sappers were brought in, one, the youngest lad of the troop, had been shot several times. I placed the poor lad in my Jeep, telling the driver, Tich Bader, to cross the bridge and take the casualty as quickly as possible to a Mobile Dressing Station (MDS) several miles out of Wetteren. A little later, still in the dark, Tich returned with the wounded lad, saying he couldn't find a way out of the town. The casualty was now asking for me, so Dicky Turpin ordered me to get him urgent medical attention. With the aid of a local civilian, we managed to find our way out of the town by travelling back the way we had come in the afternoon before. After a while we found what we were looking for in the darkness, on the side of the road, the MDS sign lit up in an upturned petrol can. I drove up the drive to a large building with this young lad sprawled across my lap and still losing blood. We got him into the building and to the on-duty Medical Officer only to find that he had just died.

Back at troop headquarters I was reporting the sad news when the enemy attacked again, almost overrunning our forward positions. However, Cpl Crutchley took a Bren gun and dashed forward firing from the hip which completely disorganised the enemy attack and forced them to withdraw. Unfortunately he was hit by a bullet in the head and fell in the open, so Lt Bob Warren, the troop second in command, took the recce car forward and drove it round in front of where L/Cpl Crutchley lay. Whilst he gave covering fire his recce corporal, Cpl Stuckfield and Lt Turpin dashed forward and pulled the wounded man to safety.

Shortly after this the enemy started shelling the bridge area and the town to our rear, but we could not be sure of their gun positions, so I climbed up the stone spiral steps inside the church tower and managed to spot the gun flashes, before beating a hasty retreat down the steps again as the tower received some direct hits! The enemy next opened up with mortar fire and again we were unsure of their location. Lt Turpin went up to 3 Section, to take personal command and to direct their fire. Unfortunately a mortar bomb landed in the section position causing several casualties, Lt Turpin lost a leg and three others were wounded. The next mortar bomb caused even more casualties, virtually writing off the section. Lt Turpin gave orders to find medical attention for his men, saying that a civilian doctor was in attendance at the convent on the south side of the river. These casualties were evacuated under heavy enemy fire with the exception of one sapper, who was rushed into the cellar of a nearby house for safety and left with the women and children who were sheltering there. The enemy were now attacking in greater strength, also their snipers were very active, keeping us pinned down. It

Plaque presented to the citizens of Ghent by the Desert Rats.

looked as if we were going to be completely over-run and were being driven back house by house. Lt Warren had taken command by now and did a great job directing our fire and forming new defensive positions, but we were really fighting for our lives. Cpl Stuckfield was doing magnificent work with his Bren gun and rallied the defence heedless of personal danger. He moved from house to house firing at the enemy from the hip and it was chiefly due to his courage and determination that their attacks were broken up.

I made an attempt to recover the man from the cellar before it was over-run by the enemy, but the fire, chiefly from snipers, made it impossible. Just as things were looking really bad, a troop of tanks from the 5DG arrived. Lt Bob Warren placed them in position and I dashed forward with one of the tanks and brought back the injured sapper from the cellar. He was also taken to the convent for medical attention.

Things were looking a little brighter now, we had some tanks for support and the houses on the far side of the sports ground where the remaining enemy were located were now under intense fire from our guns. Corporal Stuckfield with 1 Section, some men of Troop headquarters and a sergeant from the anti-tank gun crew, now worked their way in a right flanking movement up to the houses, under the covering fire of the tanks and the recce car and assaulted, wounding two Germans who were in the garden. The majority of the rest of the Jerries were in the cellars and asked to surrender. The first man came out with his hands up, but as the second came out he threw a stick grenade, which fortunately hit the ceiling and did no damage. Meanwhile Lt Warren brought up 2 Section and some men of 3 Troop and we cleared the whole area. In the back of the houses we found twenty-two Germans and nine more were taken from the cellars. These were sent back to Squadron Headquarters. Three heavy mortars were also captured in the garden.

At this point, a company of the Queens arrived, and we combined forces and attacked the final enemy strong point in a powder factory, which was on fire from our earlier efforts. The tanks gave covering fire and the whole area was cleared. A further twenty eight prisoners were captured including the company commander and the pay clerk.

The OC then recalled the troop and we consolidated in our original positions. The infantry returned and thickened up our defences. The time was then about 1500 hours on the 6th. No further trouble occurred after this.'

Aftermath

The story does not end there, for Eric Morrall was destined to meet the brave inhabitants of Wetteren again:

'It had always been my wish to return one day to Wetteren to see if I could recognise any parts of the town which holds such vivid memories for me. An opportunity came my way in August 1970 when my wife Jennie, and I were driving to Germany to spend a holiday with our daughter, Deirdre. So, whilst on the way between Ostend and Brussels, we drove a few miles off our route to visit Wetteren, planning to briefly look around for about half an hour.

Above: A Comet tank of A Squadron 5 RTR outside the Town Hall, Ghent on the first anniversary of the liberation September 6th, 1945. 'From' Fromont is one of the crew (left rear).

Another view close to the bridge in Wetteren.

On arrival in the centre of the town, I asked a Belgian youth if he spoke English and he led me a few yards to his parents' cafe where his mother, Mrs Gisella van de Velde, who spoke good English, invited us in for a chat. After this, we made our way back to our car when we saw a man walking briskly towards us. He introduced himself in very good English as Gustaaf van den Berge, another cafe owner, who had spotted the Desert Rat badge on my car. He asked the purpose of my visit to Wetteren and I said I just wished to see the town again, since I had been there briefly during the war. Once he knew the purpose of our visit, we were invited into his cafe, where we continued our talk over a cup of coffee. During our conversation he said he was about 14 years old when the town was liberated and he mentioned that the British Royal Engineers had been one of the first units to enter Wetteren and then had a battle on their hands to liberate the town from the enemy.

At my request we visited a spot on the other side of the canal where several 1 Troop lads were killed. I located the very spot, showing Gustaaf shrapnel and shrapnel marks still in the side of a house. I then recognised another house where our wounded had been put in the cellar for attention. Gustaaf made enquiries from the lady of the house, who said that they had no cellar, so with that I thought I must have been mistaken. Then this lady's husband appeared at the doorway. He said they had a cellar during the war, but that it had been filled in for safety reasons just after the war. Strangely enough this man asked Gustaaf questions about me and said he had seen me before. So we questioned each other using Gustaaf as an interpreter. He said he was only 13 years old at the time of the fighting when he lived in the cellar of this house with his mother and grandmother. He could remember me coming to the cellar to remove the wounded at the height of the battle.

After this most surprising meeting, we set off to visit the "Kliniek" (Hospital) known to me in 1944 as "The Convent", where a young Belgian doctor and several nuns did wonderful work caring for our wounded, even performing amputations in the middle of the night, also taking care of our dead comrades. On entering the hospital with Jennie, Gustaaf left us inside the main entrance, very soon to return with a nursing

84

nun; we instantly recognised each other – it was Sister Emanuel. Her first words were "You are the English Sergeant who brought your wounded comrades here during the night of the fighting". We had quite a long chat, talking about what happened to this soldier and that soldier. The sad thing was that the young doctor had since died when still quite young. The last I saw of Sister Emanuel during the war, before moving on, was when I was requested to return to the "Kliniek" to identify our dead comrades and good friends, my lads of 1 Troop.

To Gustaaf and Jennie all this was becoming unbelievable, the brief story which I had mentioned only an hour or so earlier, was now unfolding with remarkable evidence. Gustaaf was flabbergasted to think I could remember and select this particular house with the cellar, also remember other points and places of interest after so many years had passed and with the rebuilding of all damaged buildings. Now we were taken back to Gustaaf's cafe to continue our talk and Jennie and I were introduced to several other friends, so our intended half-an-hour's visit developed into an overnight stay as guests of Gustaaf and his family.

Later on I had the pleasure of meeting a young man by the name of Jacques de Vos, an historian, who was obtaining material for a book he was writing about events which took place during the war in the area of Wetteren and Ghent. He said he knew of a Sergeant Morrall of the Royal Engineers, by name only, through a British military book he possessed, which gave an account of the defence and liberation of Wetteren in 1944. Jacques produced the book – Yes! this was it. I did not know it existed, this is still more unbelievable I thought, so I produced my passport to prove to him that I was the ex-Sergeant he was hoping to meet.

Some time after returning home from our holiday, I received an invitation to attend Wetteren's Armistice Church Service on November 11th, 1970. I replied saying that I would do my utmost to attend and on November 10th I left home for Wetteren, informing Gustaaf only a couple of days in advance that I was coming. He was most kind and met me at the railway station in Ghent. Little did I know what the following day had in store for me. It was a most memorable day – a day I shall never, never forget. The photographs show some of the events.

The Last Post being played by the band of Wetteren's Fire Brigade.

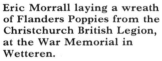

Eric Morrall laying a wreath of Flanders Poppies from the Christchurch British Legion, at the War Memorial in Wetteren.

Programme of Events on November 11/12th 1970 in brief:

08.30 Parade formed up at the Railway Station, consisting of: The Mayor and Members of the Council, Town Band, Fire Brigade and Wetteren's Legionnaires.

08.45 March through the town to the church in the Market Square.

09.15 Laying of Wreaths

09.45 Church Service

10.30 March Past

11.00 Presentation by the Mayor in his Council Chambers

12.00 Champagne Party at Mr L. Van Laey's house

13.00–17.30 Presentation Lunch with the Legionnaires.

19.00 Private Dinner Party (guest of Mr and Mrs Van Laeys)

21.30–02.30 Party at Gustaaf's Cafe.

The end of a most memorable day with very hospitable and friendly people, many whom I am pleased and proud to call my friends. Gustaaf being one of the Very Best, always out to do someone a good turn of a helping hand, a really wonderful chap.

Each year ever since on Armistice Day, I have returned to join my many Belgian friends in paying homage to our fallen comrades. To lay a wreath of "Flanders" poppies on the town's Cenotaph, whilst the "Last Post" is played by the buglers of the Fire Brigade, followed by the one minute's silence, is a very touching and memorable moment. All these ceremonies and parades have a large following led by the Mayor and with members of the Belgian Parliament, the Town Council and officials, representatives from various organisations and departments, with of course a large contingent of ex-service members, the Legionnaires complete with brass band and colourful banners. The dignity and sincerity of the people of Wetteren and their remembrance of the fallen British soldiers is really wonderful. To see the "Flame of Peace" brought forward to the Cenotaph, brought specially from The Unknown Warrior's Tomb in Westminster

Left: Visiting the graves of members of 4th Field Squadron who died in the defence of Wetteren and are buried at the British War Cemetery, Heverlee, near Brussels.

Below: 'Nurse Nightingale' – Sister Emanuel, who is now matron of the hospital at Wetteren and who did such wonderful work looking after the wounded during the battle.

Abbey, makes one feel proud as well as humble.

The next day, I also find very touching as with the help of my very good friend, Jacques de Vos, I visit the British War Cemetery at Heverlee, situated in a beautiful area to the south east of Brussels, to lay a Remembrance cross and poppies on the graves of my comrades, killed in action in the defence and liberation of Wetteren.

In 1971 on one of my visits, I had great pleasure in presenting to the Mayor and the people of Wetteren, a plaque, on behalf of the ex 4th Field Squadron RE, which I made myself and bearing my treasured RE cap badge, which I wore at the time of Wetteren's liberation. Also in 1974 I made another plaque to present to Sister Emanuel (now the Matron of Wetteren's Hospital) better known as "The Angel of Wetteren", to show our appreciation for her wonderful help in attending to our wounded comrades.

To me it is always a great pleasure to return for this special occasion and to be with such generous and good friends.'

Holland~Winter Operations

Men of 9th Battalion, The
Durham Light Infantry,
fighting in the village of
Bakenhoven, the first village
to be taken in the attack on
January 16th, 1945.

Right: Members of the Tank
Troop of Tac HQ 7th
Armoured Division taken in
Holland during the winter
1944/45.

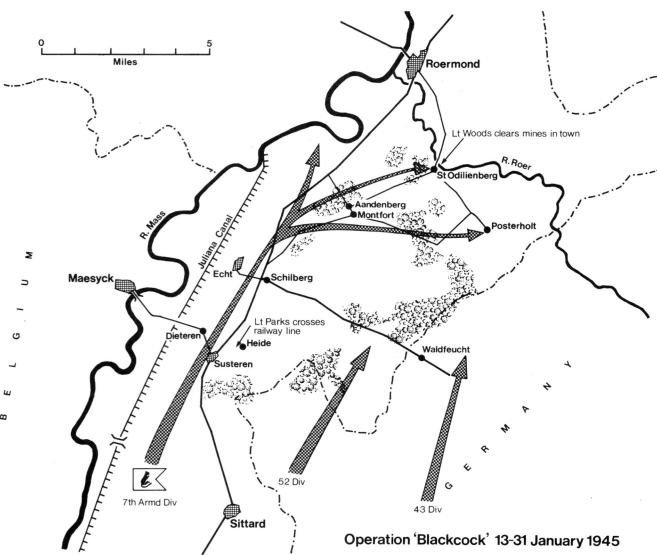

Operation 'Blackcock' 13-31 January 1945

Reorganisation of the Division

In November 1944 the Division was reorganised. 131 Lorried Infantry Brigade lost both the 1st/6th and 1st/7th Queens in exchange for the 2nd Battalion, The Devonshire Regiment and the 9th Battalion, The Durham Light Infantry, both from 50th Division. Also the Division changed commanders and General Verney, who had been GOC since August 4th, 1944, was succeeded by General L O Lyne, DSO. 'Lou' Lyne continued to command the Desert Rats for the remainder of the war.

The Victory of the Roer Triangle – Operation 'Blackcock' (January 16th–24th, 1945)

One of the essential preparations before the final drive to the Rhine was the clearing of the area between the Rivers Maas (Meuse) and Roer by 12 Corps (7th Armoured, 52nd and 43rd Divisions) in an offensive operation called 'Blackcock'. The area, known as the Roer Triangle, was held by two strong German Divisions with at least 160 guns, their defensive positions being both heavily mined and well camouflaged. The weather was dreadful; bitterly cold, snow and ice, indeed the operation had to be delayed for twelve hours due to dense fog – caused by a smoke screen, which had been put down to cover movement on the left flank, freezing in the air!

The Division opened its attack on January 16th and there followed nine days of very fierce fighting before the Triangle was finally cleared. To illustrate the battle I have chosen two excellent sketches from contemporary issues of the *Illustrated London News*, together with two accounts of the action written by troop leaders in 1 RTR and 5 Innis DG.

Alan Parks, now a Lieutenant Colonel commanding HQ Rheindahlen Garrison in the British Army of the Rhine, was then a troop leader in C Squadron 1 RTR.

'During the early part of January 1945 the 1st Royal Tank Regiment had been resting when it became clear that something was afoot. The weather was extremely cold and there was snow about. Each tank was issued with some whitewash and the crews were told to paint their vehicles with it as camouflage. There was not enough whitewash to go round, and this, plus a shortage of brushes, made it an interesting task.

On about January 16th, we were told that the Regiment was to take part in 'Operation Blackcock' which was intended to clear the remaining Germans from the triangle formed by the Rivers Roer and the Maas. A quick look at the map told us that it was rather unattractive tank country with woods, small fields and ditches with plenty of water. On January 18th the Regiment attacked and took Susteren. It was bitterly cold, the tanks slid about on the ice and there was very little protection for the crews. It was a long and tedious day but by nightfall we were in the town which was being shelled by the enemy. As it was intended to push on up the main road to Echt and Schilberg the following day, we all went for orders after dark. On returning I was extremely hungry but as there were no fires I had to be content with a cold tin of M and V (meat and veg) which my gunner handed to me – there were no electric boiling vessels on tanks in those days.

One of the Signals' lorries of Div HQ in Echt in January 1945. Note the slogan left by the retreating German forces.

The gallant fight at Susteren. B Company 1/5 Queens hanging on grimly in the northern part of Susteren village as they waited for 1st Royal Tanks to get across the Vloed Beek to support them. They were attacked by a battalion of infantry supported by six tanks, but managed to knock out two of them and to hold on until our tanks arrived. (Reproduced by kind permission of the Illustrated London News).

The first spoonful gave me quite a shock as the contents were frozen solid and did not really go down terribly well!

My orders were to take my troop and capture a small village called Heide, just to the east of Susteren and across a railway line. This was to be done at the same time as A and B Squadrons were moving north to Echt and Schilberg. We slept very little that night because of the cold and by first light I was approaching the railway ready for a quick dash through a tunnel under the line which led straight into the village. We were on our own with no infantry, so our intention was to go hell for leather down the lane running through the village. I was surprised when my point tank suddenly came to a grinding halt at the entrance to the tunnel and the commander waved his arms as if something was wrong. A quick look showed me that the whole of the subway under the line was flooded and quite impassable. There seemed nothing for it but to cross over the line on top, so I rushed at the embankment and suddenly found that I was on the line with a vast open space all around me. I realised that I was very vulnerable to any enemy in the area, so decided that I would cross over the line as quickly as possible with my other tanks following. It was an interesting and unusual sensation with the tank tracks catching in the railway lines and me wondering if they would break. Luckily due to the age of our vehicles the tracks were stretched and we soon found

ourselves roaring down the far embankment into the comparative safety of an orchard south of the village. Not a living soul or animal was in sight and the thatch of the odd farmhouse was burning merrily as we raced down the village street and took up our posts at the far end. We were pleased to be joined by some infantry shortly afterwards which gave us the opportunity for a long-overdue meal and a brew up.

Subsequently, after Echt and Schilberg had been captured, we moved on towards Posterholt which dominated the River Roer. From a tank man's point of view it was not a great battle, but the closeness of the country offered protection to the enemy and this exercised one's judgement and tactics. Rearguards were left in the form of the odd SP or anti-tank gun together with mining of the roads. One had to be especially alert and all members of the crew played their own vital part. It is interesting to remember that it was my driver, who although driving fast down a road, spotted a string of mines laid across it; pressed hard on the brakes thereby causing the tank to stand on its nose but undoubtedly saved all our lives'.

Another troop leader who took part in Operation 'Blackcock' was Henry Woods, now a Brigadier, who was then commanding 4th Troop in C Squadron of the 'Skins' (5th Royal Inniskilling Dragoon Guards).

'During the Christmas period the Division held their sector with 131 Lorried Infantry Brigade garrisoning the villages on the old Dutch/German border as a line of stray outposts. Elements of the armoured regiments also took part as infantry; B Sqn, 5 Innis DG, garrisoned Susteren/Papenhaven for a week and my troop spent one of the coldest nights I can ever recall as an infantry guard on a bridge site beside the Juliana Canal, the bridge being a jumble of twisted snow-covered steel which disappeared into the ice on the surface of the canal. When the sun rose, red rimmed in the morning, we were numb with cold, and sober, despite the consumption of a jar of rum among twelve men throughout the night. It was a very bitter winter and houses and barns were used for cover and warmth wherever we went. The infantry of the Division started the attack on January 16th, a process of classic "crumbling" to gain the German outpost villages opposite our own. It was not until January 22nd that 5 Innis DG were ordered to advance through the infantry to seize the important road junction town of Montfort, more or less in the middle of the salient, after spending a week at Susteren guarding the right flank of the left hand thrust astride the Sittard-Roermond road. The orders to the Regiment also said that 1/5th Queens would come under command late on January 22nd, to assist the advance and consolidate the gains. A and B Squadrons, each with a motor rifle platoon of A Coy 1 RB, a sapper section and a Valentine scissors bridge, moved off on two axes, B on the left towards Aandenburg and A on the right towards Montfort. C Squadron moved in reserve to the area of Echt. The wind was still bitter and the landscape of black trees in stark contrast to the white snow, appeared gloomy and malevolent. Our column jerked forward in fits and starts, reaching the Echt area soon after dark.

The left forward squadron were already closely engaged with the enemy in Aandenburg, a small village commanding the north approach of any enemy reinforcements to Montfort. The German parachutists who faced us were fighting skilfully and contesting every advance with grim determination, especially the British move into Aandenburg. It was clear that, for the time being anyway, this was the critical area, and our CO, Lt Col Swetenham, lost no time in pushing forward reinforcements to B Sqn. The rest of A Coy 1 RB, and the remaining troops of B Squadron were got forward but still the situation in Aandenburg was touch and go. Not until close on midnight did the 1/5th Queens arrive at Echt, and with great haste A Coy was mounted on C Squadron tanks to be moved to an area as close to Aandenburg as possible without becoming involved in the battle. There were enough tanks there already, and the need was for infantry to cope with the street battle.

The infantry clung on as best they could, looking very cold and miserable, even though the ones on the engine decks were warmer than they had been for many days and nights. The column of tanks without lights, and under a fitful moon often hidden by clouds, lurched into the night along an inferior shell-pocked road through St Frost. This place had been the scene of a short, sharp fight earlier in the day, and amid smouldering houses lay the wreckage of a Rifle Brigade Bren carrier (of the Scout Platoon) and a half-track, as well as a German half-track with four heavy anti-aircraft machine guns

Below: Preparations for Op Blackcock. Crews whitewashing their vehicles to match the snow – not easy with a shortage of both brushes and whitewash!

Bottom: Moving up for Op Blackcock. Tanks of the Division move up complete with whitewash to blend with the snow.

Top: The artificial moonlight battle for Montfort. Tanks and infantry of the Division attacking Montfort seized the outskirts but came up against fierce enemy resistance. The village was eventually occupied during the night of January 23rd/24th, 1945. (Reproduced by kind permission of the Illustrated London News).

Above: Troops of 2nd Battalion, The Devonshire Regiment clearing the town of Echt of German rearguards, January 18th, 1945.

mounted on it. From St Frost our route took us along a forest track, the low branches of the trees which swept over the heads of tank commanders and operators, proving an additional and nerve-wracking hazard to the infantry. In a thin wood about a mile from Aandenburg the column halted and the weary infantry clambered down, soon to disappear into the darkness towards the glow which, with the regular but intermittent crackle and explosion of small arms, grenades, mortars and shells, showed where the fight was at its height.

Meanwhile, for what was left of the night, C Sqn remained in position, peering anxiously to the north, and thus ready to secure the left flank, and our lines of communication to the Montfort/Aandenburg area. In the morning, and in company with A Coy 1 RB, C Sqn carried out a limited advance on the

same flank in support of the attack on Montfort carried out by 5 RTR and another battalion of 131 Lorried Infantry Brigade. The tanks and infantry moved forward slowly, as due to the wooded and close nature of the country, with more small fields and groups of farm buildings, it was not easy to deploy, or when the enemy resisted, to bring full fire support to bear. However, in our case there was little enemy resistance.

On January 26th the advance to the Roer continued, and C Sqn were ordered to advance at first light from the Montfort area to St Odibenburg on the Roer itself. We were led by two troops of Recce Squadron and the scout platoon of A Coy 1 RB, on whom the brunt of that day's activities fell. By late afternoon it was clear that an enemy rearguard was well ensconced, aided by extensive minefields around the town. A formal attack was laid on for the following morning, in which the advance was led by two troops of Flails from the Lothian and Border Horse and C Squadron, together with a company of 2 Devons, advanced on the right towards the town. The Flails moved off over the Start Line, about 600m from the first houses, with artillery and tank covering fire, and successfully breached the minefield. 1st and 4th Tps of C Squadron then moved through, with the Devons, and while 1st Tp went straight towards the centre of the town, my 4th Tp swung right down to the road running into the town along the banks of the Roer River.

The infantry slipped quickly along the street, using all the cover, from garden to garden, house to house, room to room, and, with my tank leading, we followed along the road, taking advantage of what cover there was from garden walls. I had not gone more than 200m, when I observed, at the same time as my driver, that the next 100m of road had many little hummocks of snow. That instant we realised that these were mines, and the armoured element halted. Attempts to contact the Devon's platoon on the separate tank/infantry radio were not successful, and so the platoon went on ahead before we could warn them of our (and as it turned out their) predicament. Having reported the reason for delay, I dismounted myself, my driver and co-driver, and ordered the driver and co-driver of the next tank (my Tp Sgt) to come too. On scraping away the snow, we found the dreaded Schu-mines – anti-personnel rather than anti-tank – underneath. We therefore, cleared a gap one tank wide and returned to move the troop through the gap. Meanwhile, enemy mortars and machine guns on the east bank of the river Roer had reacted to our presence and the operation of clearing the mines, in which the rear platoon of the Devons had now joined, was not without adventure. The Germans could see and shoot between the houses, and the infantry had I think two casualties from this fire. It is strange how even in a cumbersome tank winter oversuit one could run at high speed when the Spandaus spoke.

At length the troop moved forward and rejoined the leading Devons platoon in the centre of the town, at the same time meeting the leading tank of 1st Troop which had driven into the town from the south west. It was now plain that the German rearguard, minus a few dead, a few casualties and a small group of very sullen prisoners, had escaped across the river. As we watched the black waters of the Roer sliding past the houses at the end of the street, even an ordinary troop leader could tell that this operation was over. At last we could hope to return to warm barns and houses away from the bitter cold for a short while. We did not of course know that Operation Blackcock was to be our only winter campaign and that our next operation would be across the Rhine itself in the early spring'.

Soon after the successful completion of the Blackcock operation, the Corps Commander, General Ritchie, wrote to GOC Seventh Armoured Division and said:

'I cannot tell you how I admire the really dogged and fine fighting qualities the Division has displayed throughout "Blackcock". Yours was the most important role, for unless you created the breach, the operations could not have developed so well as they did. The Division did many really good things in this operation, but none which I admire more than the determined fighting spirit displayed by both armour and infantry in the operations leading up to the securing of Echt; operations forced through by hard fighting to a successful conclusion in the most adverse conditions of weather in which Blackcock started'.

The Desert Rats certainly had every reason to be satisfied with their efforts. They had destroyed one German division, badly mauled a crack paratroop battle group and gained all their objectives. They could now enjoy a brief rest period before the battle for Germany itself began.

Below: Two surprised Germans are caught in the village of Dieteren by a soldier of 9 DLI, January 16th, 1945.

Bottom: Men of 9 DLI moving through Schilberg together with a column of Churchill tanks January 20th, 1945. Some Churchills were fitted with a flame gun in place of the bow machine gun. The 'Crocodile', as it was called, was a fearsome weapon capable of directing accurately a stream of burning fluid for about 90 yards.

Continental
Living

War-torn buildings provided some shelter, although these Riflemen preferred to eat outside.

Where the Living was Easy

It might be imagined by those who fought only in the empty inhospitable deserts of North Africa or the dripping jungles of Burma, that the advantages of combat in civilised surroundings were considerable. But it was not so, civilians are out of place on a battlefield and quickly become homeless refugees. Buildings are reduced to piles of impenetrable rubble prohibiting constructive movement, indeed, the very pattern of civilisation hinders the whole business of war.

What was it like to fight in Europe? I hope that the photographs on the following pages will give some idea of how the Desert Rats fared in their new surroundings.

Homes Various

An armoured division is by definition a mobile formation, constantly on the move, so the vast majority of Desert Rats continued to make their vehicles their homes as they had done so before in the Desert. From time to time it was possible to use buildings but never for very long in any one place.

Food Glorious Food

The introduction of the composite ration pack was probably the most useful addition provided for the Army by the Supply branch, because it made certain that, on most days

anyway, every soldier could be guaranteed an adequate, appetising and balanced meal, whether he was in or out of action. The proposal to produce ration packs originated with the BEF in 1939 and by the end of the war most of our Allies were producing similar rations.

Keeping Clean and Tidy

As anyone who has done any camping will tell you the open air life make you lose your inhibitions especially as to where you perform such everyday acts as bathing or having a haircut.

Top left: Some ruins took on a strange beauty such as can be seen in this striking photograph of Aunay-sur-Odon near Mt Pincon in Normandy.

Above: Happy smiles all round on the faces of these French women and children who have just been liberated by the Skins.

Top right: Dead and bloated cattle were another unsavoury feature of war in a civilised environment.

Above: A tank harbour in daylight. Not a manoeuvre to be attempted for any length of time without air superiority, however, on occasions it was essential for refuelling, replenishment or reorganisation.

Miscellany

The photographs which follow are a mixture of people, places and animals which, I believe, speak for themselves in portraying some of the good and some of the bad aspects of soldiering in Europe.

Beer, Glorious Beer!

So that we keep the proper perspective in this survey of Continental living, I have included some photographs dedicated to that most serious subject dear to the hearts of all Desert Rats – strong drink, for example; beer, vino or even zbib. The latter was a lethal, inflammable, corrosive and explosive beverage, popular in Sergeants' Messes. It was normally 95 per cent wood alcohol and burned with a fierce blue flame.

The Charlie Love

Finally, to close this short account of life in war torn Europe, here is a description of that strange phenomenon known as 'The Charlie Love':

'The expression "Charlie Love" (in other words the "Centre Line") wasn't in vogue much in the Desert, because there was no restriction to one's movement. "C" Squadron, Eleventh Hussars, of course, did have a field day on the Bardia–Tobruk road in June 1940, but this was merely classed as an ambush. It is, however, worthy of note, because in present times it would class as a Gold Cup winner. Another important feature was that throughout the early stages of the war it was played the wrong way round; on this occasion the bag was ninety puggled Wop Met, (Mixed Enemy Transport) and their occupants, a real live general, the local outpost brothel truck, with three women, and an officer, his wife, who was heavy with child, and the nurse, who immediately drank a bottle of iodine, but had to give it back again owing to the sharpness of the medical orderly. The next opera-

Members of Div HQ Staff (tank crews and signallers) make themselves at home in a half-destroyed house in Echt, Holland.

tion was at Sidi Saleh, which produced an even larger bag.

On neither of these occasions was the way for the enemy restricted. There was unlimited desert to go on and the success of the performance was due to the helplessness of the Italians and their refusal to leave the only road that existed.

I give these examples to remind you that this new and interesting game, known throughout the Army as "chewing up the Charlie Love" was only a concentrated form of "smartening up the loha". Like many other things, it appeared in its true light in Europe.

The game consists of two parties – Ours and Theirs. We always make the first move (because they make the necessary counter-measures preventing the game being reversed): this consists of pushing our chin well out into the virgin country up front, where there seem to be no enemy. When nicely placed and everyone is "brewing up", they move in behind us and prepare to put in the bag the SQMS, the Echelon, RHQ DR and the odd Tech Armd Car (with only a driver) which are bumming down the Charlie Love, their occupants nodding in peaceful slumber.

The first staccato burst of Spandau, or the sickening thud of HE wakens the dreamers, and from that moment things begin to move sharpish. Milling sets in as they try to turn round (except for the water truck, which opens the throttle and pushes on into the bag), and there are collisions, and vehicles at all angles across the road, many of which can't face the pressure any longer and subside, groaning, into the ditch.

The true situation is, of course, not known at RHQ, who merely state that the echelon must be held up by traffic blocks. The news of the chewing arrives by rumour first. Someone was talking to a water-truck driver who said there were a hundred Tigers chewing up the Charlie Love, and that out of forty vehicles all were "brewed" except himself, and he only escaped because, as luck would have it, the brakes wouldn't work (the Tech hadn't got any fluid) and he was out the other side before things really got going. This rumour gets stronger as each new arrival comes in. The enemy force grows to an army corps, and the devastation to the most fantastic proportions. Nothing more is heard until, sensing that there must be something up, a troop is sent back down the Charlie Love to investigate. Yes, it's true, there are Moffer (German soldiers) messing about fifteen miles back. And so it goes on.

The first match was played within seventy-

Above: These White half tracks belonging to 65th Anti-Tank Regiment (Norfolk Yeomanry) are parked outside a very desirable residence, the local pub!

Centre left: This 'saloon' bodied half track was specially built up by 1 RHA, REME for the Signals Section – the proud 'owner' (C Davis) told me that he once did 45mph in it!

Bottom left: Another 'home on wheels' in Normandy, 1944.

Left: Most vehicle convoys would try to get under the cover of hedgerows etc and take advantage of natural camouflage to augment vehicle camouflage nets.

Top: 'If you know a better 'ole, go to it!' Looking reminiscent of Bruce Bairnsfather's World War I character Old Bill, these soldiers of 1 RB make the best of very difficult living conditions.

two hours of landing in Normandy, on the Villers Bocage–Briquessard road. The chewing lasted about fourteen hours, but as both sides were inexperienced, only one lorry was "brewed". The second round was at Oudenarde, where the enemy were treated as conquering heroes by the flag-waving and flower-throwing civies, until the latter were soundly trounced by machine-gun fire, which was how the SS often introduced themselves.

The greatest chew of all came on the only road between the troops at Nijmegen and Eindhoven. For miles lorries were lying three abreast waiting for someone to remove the enemy so that they could get on. On this occasion it took a large part of the division to clear the Charlie Love and four tanks were destroyed. The scene on the road showed it had been a good match. About fifteen

lorries were "brewed up" and a Sherman tank. This was the biggest match played, as latterly it has consisted of "brewing up" the OP places with bazookas, and other rather childish things.

The Charlie Love, I should explain, is the road, probably the only road usable, which must carry all the soft stuff as well as tanks, transporters, and so on. In most cases, whether out of the amusement it affords to the onlooker in a jeep or out of ignorance, the Charlie Love seldom is a road where you can pass another car without drawing in your elbows and knees. Often it is a cart track with 2-foot deep boggy ruts, caused by the tanks, and everyone gets stuck. When the Charlie Love is well established, many painted signs appear, such as "When in doubt BREW UP"; "If you must stop, get off the road" and then a little later, "If you can't get off the road, don't stop" (even if all the tyres are flat!) At bridges you get "Step on it if you want to live" (when under fire) and in one place "Russians! Don't Shoot!"

Yes, the Charlie Love produces a host of interesting views. Now there are no more of them, and the only time we get chewed up on a road is for proceeding at 30.2 mph in England. This will cost you a fiver and your licence endorsed, and there will be nothing funny about it either, because you won't have a fiver, and thus will be going to the "cooler" for a week. When you come out you'll be courtmartialled for going AWOL! Such is life".*

*First published in the Victory Number of the Eleventh Hussar Journal and reprinted here by kind permission of Home Headquarters, The Royal Hussars.

Far left, top: Unpacking Composite Rations – The 'Compo' ration pack was designed to give a good breakfast, a dinner and a substantial evening meal, plus some items which could be used as snacks during the day. There were seven types of packs which included such firm favourites as rice pudding, mixed-fruit pudding, red salmon and tinned fruit. Cigarettes, matches and soap were also included.

Far left, centre: The contents of 'Compo' packs was designed to be eaten cold if no means of heating was available. However, all AFVs carried small cookers (two seen here in right foreground). The enamelled white coffee pot must have been a treasured item 'acquired' en route to Berlin!

Far left, bottom: Armoured soldiers clearly had to be able to eat their meals on the move, as demonstrated by these tank crewmen of the Skins.

Left: General 'Lou' Lyne, GOC of the Division, takes tea with some of his officers in 'A' Mess in a Dutch farmhouse near Echt, Holland, January 1945.

Left: Cows to milk. Cows which happened to still be alive in the battle area were fair game (can you see the bucket?)

Above: Bath time in a tank leaguer.

Top right: Sheep to steal. It is anybody's guess where this 'Prisoner of War' finished up!

Right: A haircut 'in the field' for Commander R Signals, 7th Armoured Division.

Above left: Whiskey, friend and companion of the late Douglas Boggie, Norfolk Yeomanry, posing on his 'Kennel'.

Above centre: This enthusiastic supporter of 'Compo' ration packs containing Grade 3 salmon unfortunately got stuck in the tin and had to be helped out!

Centre left: Amateur musicians of 22nd Armoured Brigade Workshops 'at play' – (note the bicycle strategically placed for a quick getaway if anyone complains of the noise!)

Bottom left: George Formby and his 'Uke' entertaining the troops in his own inimitable manner.

Top right: Mind my Bike!

Right: Well armed members of 22nd Armoured Brigade Workshops out hunting.

Far right: Even mundane jobs like typing orders take on a new meaning 'in the field'.

Above: Favourite pastime
of all Desert Rats!

Below: Obviously a vintage
year!

Far right: War's over, so
now we can get down to the
really serious business.

Into the Fatherland

Men of 9 DLI engaged in clearing the village of Weseke.

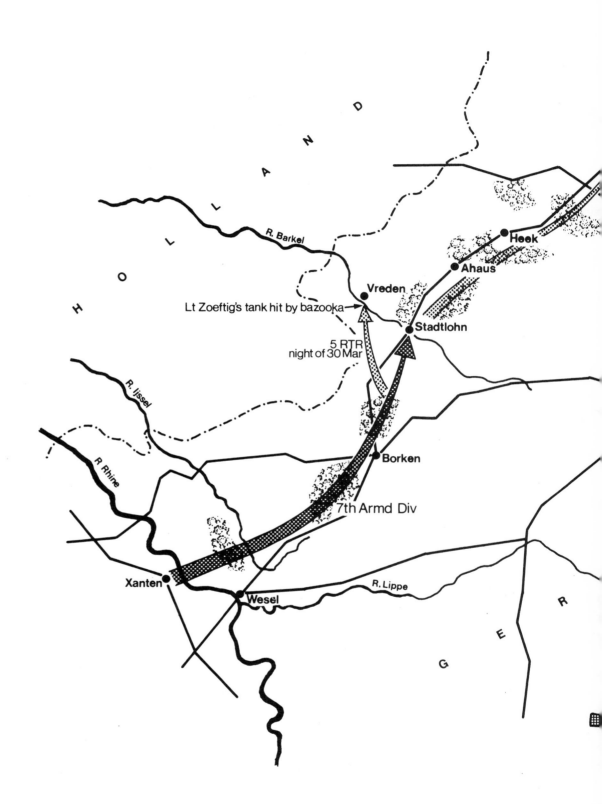

Lt Zoeftig's tank hit by bazooka

5 RTR
night of 30 Mar

Heek

Ahaus

Vreden

Stadtlohn

R. Barkel

R. Ijssel

R. Rhine

Borken

7th Armd Div

Xanten

Wesel

R. Lippe

H O L L A N D

G E R

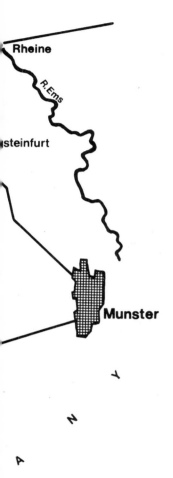

'Night Attack' Vreden 30th March 1945

Tanks in Line!
(To the tune of 'Tales from the Vienna Woods')
'Tanks, Tanks, Tanks in Line,
Sweeping, on towards the Rhine,
The First, the Fifth, the Skins and Guns
We're out to b . . . up the Huns!
Cromwells, Shermans, Fireflies too
A floating punch to see us through,
The Engineers with Scorpions
And a troop of Bofors, half a dozen loafers,
And the Navy nice and wavy,
RAF umbrella, nothing could be sweller,
Deutschland here we come!'

This was the first verse of a song which had its beginnings in the Desert days when the tanks of the Division were 'Sweeping on to Alamein'. The European version was composed in Holland during October 1944 by some officers of 'C' Squadron, 1st Royal Tank Regiment, after operations north of Tilburg. The second verse goes on:

'The First are always at the front,
"C" Squadron picked to bear the brunt,
The "iron ring" well at the back
The Sergeant Major's thrown a track,
Tom Stacey he will do the trick
But only with his usual tick.
The 95's are wanging,
88's are banging
Johnnie Dingwall slanging
Office staff are lazy
Tank Commanders hazy
It's about time that we had a brew
– Too true!'

This verse does perhaps need some explanation – The 'iron ring' refers to Squadron Headquarters; Tom Stacey was 'C' Squadron fitter sergeant, who continued to serve in the First, with distinction, for many years after the war: two of the Cromwells in SHQ were armed with 95mm howitzers instead of the normal 75mm, whilst the deadly accurate German 88mm gun was both well known and respected by all; finally Johnnie Dingwall, a famous 1 RTR character of World War 2, was then commanding 'C' Squadron. 'Tanks in Line' is still sung lustily after dinner nights in the First's officers' mess and is now as much a part of their regimental tradition as their black berets and ash plants.

Operations in Germany
In order to give some idea of the operations which the Division carried out in Germany I have chosen three stories, all by armoured soldiers, but each very different. The first concerns the feelings of a tank troop leader, Lt Ted Zoeftig of 5 RTR, during a night operation in which he was bazookered. The second is an extract from the diary, for early April 1945, of Captain Richard Brett Smith of the Eleventh Hussars and is typical of the slow progress and bitter fighting which characterised the early days of the final campaign. Finally, I have finished on a more cheerful note with the liberation of a British Prisoners of War camp near Fallingbostel, by Captain (now Brigadier) Tim Pierson of the Eighth Hussars.

Night Attack March 30th, 1945
Anyone who has driven in the dark along unfamiliar country roads knows the feeling of relief when that all important road junction which your navigator has been telling you for the past ten minutes is 'just around the next bend', finally appears and your headlights are able to pick out the strange sounding place names on the signboard. Imagine, therefore, how much more difficult it is when one is perched on top of a noisy, lurching steel monster, without lights, only able to glance furtively at your map from time to time with the aid of a flashlight, exposed to the elements and constantly on the alert for trouble. It is, I believe, one of the most severe tests of a tank commander, particularly if he is also spearheading an important advance into enemy held territory.

This was the case in the story which follows. 7th Armoured Division had crossed the Rhine a few days before near Xanten, as Corps reserve. Now they were leading on the Corps' right flank, making for an important enemy airfield complex around Rheine. There had been only minor enemy interference until Stadtlohn (see sketch map) where fierce fighting was even now taking place. A patrol of the 11th Hussars, operating on the left, managed to get to within about a thousand yards of Vreden – north of Stadtlohn, and reported that the bridge there appeared undamaged. To be able to capture Vreden and the bridge over the River Berkel would cut the enemy's line of retreat. 5th Royal Tank Regiment, with infantry support, was therefore despatched that night to capture the bridge. They set off, first moving over some bad tracks until they reached the main road, where a road block caused them some delay but was finally successfully re-

Tanks in Line! Tanks of the Division massed across the Rhine at Brunen, awaiting orders to continue the chase.

moved. Although enemy were present in the woods all round no serious opposition was encountered until the leading tank reached the outskirts of Vreden. Here it was hit by a bazooka and knocked out. The next tank was also ditched and surrounded by enemy infantry. The infantry who had been with the two tanks suffered casualties, but were able to fight their way back to the main body where a plan was made to deal with the enemy strong point. However, before this could be put into effect the enemy withdrew and 5 RTR were able to enter Vreden, only to have the enemy blow the bridge as the leading tank approached. The column then returned to Stadtlohn after destroying an enemy self-propelled gun on the far side of the river at the blown bridge.

That is the bare factual outline of this minor incident in the Division's progress through North West Europe, but it was an incident which was anything but trivial for Lieutenant Ted Zoeftig of 5 RTR, who was commanding the leading tank troop in the column and was at the receiving end of the enemy bazooka rocket. Here is his story:
'My troop was leading. Lieutenant Doug Smith was my Baker.* My Firefly (a Sherman fitted with a 17 pounder, instead of the

normal 75mm) had thrown a track about five minutes before the advance. The "A" set radio net was a bit "blabby" but since the attack was so imminent no possible harm could come of it. It certainly didn't disturb me. Some remarks were even complimentary! We had Canadian troops up on the tanks with us. We all felt comfortably confident in a subdued comradely manner. I remember agreeing the Verey signals with the Canadian officer and then lending him my Verey pistol because he didn't have one of his own. An 11th Hussar recce car purred up and had an encouraging word. "Yes, it was clear up to a small road block – No, there didn't seem to be anyone there." We paused, the "A" set chatter was dreadfully loud. No moon of course, just a clear sky with some shady warning of pre-dawn glow. "Yes! We'll come up the road block with you – *and* move it if you'll cover us". Wonderful chaps the 11th Hussars. Now we are well past the block. Over to the "B" set. "Baker – take the lead". A not exactly cheerful "Wilco – out" in reply. Head down just below the turret for a few seconds – to map read.

*A tank troop normally consisted of three tanks – the troop leader plus two others designated for use on the radio 'Able' and 'Baker'.

"We're coming up to the wood's edge. About 1 200 yards short of the little town. There's open ground after that".

I request over the "A" set to drop my infantry and work forward in concert – flushing the road as we proceed – "No", the answer comes back "You're late already, speed up if you can". I call up Douglas Smith on the "B" set. "I'll take the lead now Doug". "Roger – out". I see the blur of a shadow of small building on the right. Head down for a second to read the map – the torch doesn't seem too bright – only about 300 yards to go to the "blue" (the river), "Slow down a bit, driver". Head down for another quick glimpse of the map and there's the bridge ahead. Then a massive vibration of thick, light and dark grey lines. I feel very heavy and find that I am being pressed down to the bottom of the turret. I feel as if I'm swimming under water. In strange slow motion I start to move up. No one is near me. The tank seems to be pointing up in the air. A high pitched screaming whistle persists in my ears. I find myself sliding over the back of the engine decks to fall and roll over onto the road. There is a spitting, crackling sound – rather sharp – but not loud – round about me. One pace and I flop into a shallow ditch. A grey lump is level with my right eye. I have just tripped over

someone. Sticky feeling in my mouth. My nose is bleeding or something is. I feel all right. A sizzling sound is in front of me and what seems like lighted matches spurt up from the ground about nine inches from my head. A realisation that this is tracer, seemingly aimed directly at me, rapidly clears my sleepy thinking. But something is definitely wrong with my hearing. That machine gun is doing nothing but Squeak!

Now I realise that my tank has been heavily fired on. The Canadian troops who had clung so eagerly to the turret have scattered – one or two, probably many more, are lying on the road; my protectors in death. What had happened to my crew? Have I failed them? Where was Doug? – God – he must have got it as well! What was to have been the first firm, speedy, sure-footed thrust to the Elbe had been tripped. The machine gun stopped. I was becoming alert. I must do something – what a bloody mess. Can I get back into the tank to use the "A" set? I turn my head slowly sideways. The nose of the tank and turret seemed to appear mountainously high on the dark skyline. Must be careful or they'll see me. A dreadful sense of guilty failure is beginning to envelop me. Had I left my crew? Where were they? Still in the tank – wounded – smashed? "Do something! At least you're not afraid. Think clearly! Determined? This is

Tanks and vehicles of the Division passing through Brunen in pursuit of the enemy.

A Cromwell passing through Borken, March 30th, 1945.

easy – make a dash – ready? Now!" – Straight into a group of about eight Jerry paratroopers – all young. Their marksmanship was appalling. They missed at point blank range, but I was moving fast – straight into them, that's what spoiled their aim. Then the kicking, struggling and shouting started – but that was nothing, *anything* was better than the dreadful sense of failure. What was the waiting regiment going to do? The bitter taste of defeat and the chagrin of fallen pride remains until today.

They dragged me off – over the bridge and then blew it up – I heard something go off with a bang. Later, shortly afterwards, I got away. There seemed to be hundreds of them and they appeared rather sorry for knocking me about, as if they knew the war was finished. All I received were split eardrums, a bloody nose, split lips and a small cut on my head. I made my wobbly way back to the Regiment about three or four days later.'

Extract from the Diary of Captain Brett-Smith of the Eleventh Hussars March 31st, 1945
'Through Stadtlohn (a completely ruined and war-wrecked town, smelling horribly of death and burning) and then by country tracks to rejoin the main road, Stadtlohn-Ahaus. Apparently the 1st Tanks had made a

real cavalry charge in the night from Stadtlohn to Ahaus, and got through the hordes of bazookamen with amazingly light casualties. A terrific show and they were played out when we reached them in Ahaus.

Ahaus was also badly devastated, and there were still a few last-ditchers sniping, and a good number of mines holding up further progress. (Nigel Campbell, of D Squadron, had two Daimlers bown up). However, I was informed that the Recce Troop of 1st Tanks was through Ahaus and pushing on, so I told Van (Major W V Burdon, MC, my Squadron Leader in "C") this and followed them up. About half a mile out I met an RHA OP, who told me to move off a bridge I was on, which was being shelled every five minutes, and directed me on to the tanks (two Honeys) who were just a little way on. As I came up to them they were firing spasmodically at the woods on both sides of the main road, which was banked up on each side. One of the Honeys had to turn back for more gas, so I left Sgt Palmer and the others well back, as I expected trouble, and closed up the first Honey, telling the troop leader that I would follow him at about thirty yards and watch the left. Actually I volunteered to take over the lead and the patrol, as I thought it my duty, though it was his show, and after a

good-natured argument we agreed that I should do this when we got to a certain point. We never did, and I still have rather a guilty conscience about it. We met in Berlin after the war, and he was most generous and kind about it, and we had quite a party to celebrate his and our escape.

Sure enough, we had not gone more than another 300 yards down this very straight road, when an anti-tank gun at the end of it opened up, and brewed the Honey with its first shot. Simultaneously bazookas on the left of the road fired at him and me, and I reversed sharpish. By the grace of God the Honey made so much smoke and such a good brew-up that the German gunners were unsighted: but five or six 88mm AP shots whistled past very close to my Daimler, and caused considerable consternation amongst the half tracks and some more tanks further back! Mercifully we got off the road after a hectic bit of reversing into a farmhouse forecourt, then I collected the troop and sat in observation. The troop leader of the Honeys had got out with his operator – as I had seen, but the driver was killed. We crawled up the ditches on both sides of the road to get them, and were relieved and surprised to meet them returning on the way. The operator was wounded, and their own people got both

away to safety. Then I and Sgt Palmer with some of the men from the half tracks tried to get close to the 88 along the ditches, but we couldn't get close enough to spot it because of small arms fire from the wood and to our left. In any case it had probably moved already. We smartened up the likely areas with small arms but with what effect I cannot say.

I not unnaturally decided to take it very steady, and sat in observation most of the day. We got the RHA on to where we thought the gun was from the original flashes (finding out later that we were wrong, of course) and waited for the tanks to find a way cross-country. There was some heavy plough on the left but goodish going on the right. This they did very well. I had tried the plough in my Dingo, not daring to show it on the road, but very nearly got bogged down and had to give it up. They negotiated it, as I say, well, but met trouble, so were unable to go fast. Although I thought that the gun had probably baled out, I was not taking any chances. (Windy!) In the evening a mobile column composed of 1st Tanks, Crocodiles and Bren carriers swept up the road to prove that it had moved, helped by the information of the tanks who had got ahead on the right, after a sticky time in the

Left: A Cromwell passes a road block left by the enemy in Stadtlohn, March 31st, 1945.

Below: Tanks of the Division driving through Ahaus.

GERMANS FLEEING, AND DELIRIOUS BRITISH AND AMERICAN PRISONERS CHEERING FROM THE ROOFS OF THEIR PRISON HUTS, AS AN 8TH HUSSARS TANK SQUADRON
OF THE 7TH ARMOURED DIVISION ROLLS UP TO THE MAIN GATES OF STALAG 11B IN THE EARLY-MORNING LIGHT OF APRIL 16.

The Liberation of Stalag XIB drawn by Captain Bryan de Grineau. Reproduced by kind permission of the London Illustrated News.

woods. The column finished up near Heck, where we joined them.

Entry (part) for April 5th
A day of pouring rain and constant Luftwaffe attack. (Visibility too bad for RAF, and Luftwaffe only dare come up when its like this – first time since January 1st I have come up against them). To Dielingen then on to Lembricht, where 5th Tanks and RHA did very well, and took the place. Following up we took two POW (both wounded by their guns). Through the burning village and took lead while RB's were still clearing it; 4-5 mile patrol up to a railway bridge. Shortly before this a roadblock had held us up for some little time, and Sgt Palmer and myself had both been sniped by a sniper when we were least prepared for it. However, we brewed up a farm, and the Germans withdrew, assisted by the Colonel of 5th Tanks, always well up (Lt Col A R Leakey) tore down the road block after some of his tanks had had a go at it. Took four more POW on the CL. Also lost face slightly by asking the infantry to deal with a battery of AA 88's on my right, which turned out to be dummies, when I thought them merely deserted! Saw best sight of the war on this day – a Focke Wolf 190 hit its wing against the tree-tops, crashed into a field, bounced literally 200

yards and brewed. We put up considerable small arms fire against 'Schmitts and FW and I think Sgt Palmer hit one though he didn't bring it down within our sight. Unpleasant day'.

The Liberation of Stalag XI B, Fallingbostel – April 16th, 1945
Perhaps one of the happiest achievements of the Division's operations in April 1945 was the liberation of the great prison camp in the woods south west of Fallingbostel. Some prisoners had been there since the Fall of France, amongst others more recently arrived were members of 4 CLY and 'A' Company, 1 RB, who had been put into the bag at Villers Bocage nearly a year before (see 'Into the Bocage'). Newest of all was a leave party from the Norfolk Yeomanry whose truck had taken a wrong turning near Ibbenbüren only a fortnight previously! As well as British and American prisoners there were some twelve thousand other allied nationalities many of whom had suffered appalling hardships. Here is how Tim Pierson who was then commanding the reconnaissance troop of the Eighth Hussars remembers that wonderful day:

'Nosing its way cautiously along sandy tracks that skirted or went through the many pine-woods that were the main feature of this country, the leading section of Honeys started off slowly. Though there was no sign of any enemy, similar woods had produced quite a few the day before, and the leading tank occasionally raked the edges of the trees and suspicious hollows or clumps of grass to discourage any panzer-faust expert that might be waiting hopefully for us to get within range of his very useful weapon. The afternoon before, when he had been missed three times, Lieutenant Anstey, the leading tank commander, confessed to feeling like a goal-keeper in a football match, but this particular sunny morning there was, much to our relief, no sign of them.

A wide clearing confronted us, obviously man-made, cut at right angles through the woods, its sandy surface covered with tufts of grass, stretching dead straight to the right as far as we could see, and to the left turning out of sight through two small mountains of earth. This must be the autobahn, though scarcely what we had expected, the maps have given no hint of this rudimentary stage in its construction.

We turned left, came to the huge heaps of earth and halted while the leading commander, Corporal Spencer, dismounted to have a look at what lay round them out of sight. No more woods, but a flat open expanse of grass bounded, some thousand yards away, by a long uneven line of low buildings, out of which, further to our left, rose what looked like half a dozen tall warehouses. Binoculars showed that the main mass of low buildings lay behind a high wire fence – and people, at first we saw one or two moving about, then made out groups of a dozen, and finally realised that the thickening of the bottom half of the fence was in fact a solid mass of them. At this moment the leading tanks of "C" Squadron, approaching on a different route, came up behind us, and without waiting to see any more we jumped into our tanks and shot out into the open. In high spirits we crossed the grass as quickly as the ground would allow, but as the distance between us and the fence grew less we noticed that the predominant colour of the mass that was streaming out of the gates towards us was grey, dark grey. At the same moment we saw a French flag – or was it Dutch – which in our excitement we had not noticed before, fluttering behind the main gate. Our hopes sank; these were not British prisoners, but another of the camps full of all nationalities of Europe that we had come

across so many times before. Perhaps there were some British amongst them, then again perhaps there was no British camp at all, and the Germans have moved XIB as they had moved so many others out of the way of the armies advancing from east to west.

The leading tank came to a stop as the first of the breathless, shouting stream of humanity surrounded it, and Corporal Spencer, still clinging to a faint hope, lent down and yelled "English soldaten?" He repeated himself in a moment's hush and then a hundred hands pointed to his left, and the clamour of the excited crowd broke out with increased intensity. As he looked round for someone out of whom he could get some sense it seemed that every nation was represented, women as well as men, the majority in civilian clothes, with but two things in common; they were all happy, and all indescribably dirty.

Noticing one persistent man who seemed to have a smattering of English he hauled him up on to the tank and asked which way. The fellow pointed, and as the tank moved slowly forward the crowd melted away in front. He glanced over his shoulder and noticed that he was still leading, the Cromwells of "C" Squadron were as uncertain as he had been as to the route, but were now following hot on his heels. It was going to be

General 'Lou' Lyne inspects the Jordan Bridge across the River Weser at Nienburg. The bridge (a Class 40 Bailey Pontoon) was built by the Division's sappers on April 13th, 1945 and was called 'Jordan' as there appeared to be only one more river (the Elbe) to cross. In fact the very next obstacle encountered by the Division when the advance was resumed beyond the Aller was a brook called Jordan, near Kirchboizen!

Top: Headquarters 22nd Armoured Brigade at Syke, on the southern approaches to Bremen, April 1945.

Above: Divisional Headquarters staff sorting through some of the enormous numbers of maps which were required during the rapid advance through Germany.

built to carry the autobahn, but with no autobahn to carry looking comically like a piece from a child's set of toy bricks. A quick glance to the right revealed nothing more than an empty road. But the guide was tugging at Spencer's sleeve and jabbering away – and following with our eyes the direction of his pointing arm we saw across the road through a gap between two trees a khaki-clad figure wearing a maroon coloured beret, clinging to a wire fence beyond and jumping up and down, obviously shouting his head off, though not a word reached us over the noise of the engines and earphones.

And then all the way down to the right we could see between the tree-trunks more figures racing along the wire. We'd got there, and before the Cromwells, which came up behind just as we moved off down the road giving the glad news over the air. Three or four hundred yards down the road was the main gate to the camp and as we approached the sound of welcome from the crowd that lined the wire and covered the roofs of the camp buildings grew to a roar that penetrated our earphones above the noise of our engines. Inside the main gates was an open space packed with British prisoners, and beyond another wire fence, what looked like an inner enclosure was black with figures. This was Stalag XI B.

Quite staggering was the contrast between this scene and that which we had seen at other camps containing prisoners of the Allied nations. Despite the enthusiasm of the men inside you could see at a glance that here was order and discipline. The remarkable RSM Lord, Grenadier Guards, of the 1st Airborne Division had already taken charge and was busily engaged in his office giving peace-time orders to his Orderly Warrant Officers. Camp MP's, each with a red armband, policed the gates, and as the crowd came out to meet us there was no ugly rush but a steady controlled stream that surrounded each tank as it stopped, a stream wearing the headgear of what looked like every unit in the Army. The Airborne beret predominated – men of D-Day, Arnhem, even the Rhine crossing who had only been inside for a few weeks – but you could pick out the hats, caps, berets and bonnets of a score of others. And under each one was such a look of happiness and thankfulness that made us as happy to be the cause of it. It was a quiet crowd that thronged round us; they had had their cheer, and now when the moment came for words,

a close thing who reached the Camp first.

Parallel to the fence, which he had now reached, ran a concrete road, and turning left along this, to the accompaniment of cheers from the waving smiling crowd of prisoners and DPs that thronged its entire length, he soon passed the tall warehouses that had first been noticed in the distance. The fellow on the turret pointed excitedly forward, but Corporal Spencer could see nothing, except a road, tree-lined on both sides, that met ours at right angles. We halted at the junction; to our left the road went under a stone bridge few words came. Mostly they were too moved to speak, men who could only grin broadly and clasp your hand as the tears ran down their cheeks. You couldn't speak yourself, only shake as many as possible of the hands that stretched towards you, and grin back, trying to take it all in, and marvel. For these men didn't look like prisoners; the battle-dresses were pressed and clean, here and there web belts and gaiters were scrubbed white and the brasses gleaming, they might have been off duty in a town at home instead of just walking out of prison wire behind which they had been for anything from five weeks to five years.

Memories of that scene leave a picture of a healthy and, if not overfed, certainly not starving crowd, of apologetic requests for cigarettes and one man turning green with his first puff, having given up the habit for his three years inside; of the creases in the tartan trews and the shining buttons on the jacket of a CSM in the 51st Highland Division, who admitted having marched five or six hundred kilometres from East Prussia and who didn't look as if he had been more than five or six hundred yards from his own front door; of the Camp MO indignantly denying cases of typhus; of the German Commandant and a few of the camp guards standing apart in a small group watching unmoved the reversal of his role, and handing over his automatic with an offer to show us over the nearby storehouses; scraps of conversation "I've been waiting five years for this day" – "Three days ago we expected you", and in contrast, "You've come too soon, my jacket's still wet", this from one who had washed his battledress specially for the occasion; and from one as impressed by our appearance (we hadn't washed or shaved for nearly forty-eight hours) as were we by theirs. "You look like real soldiers". There were several requests to see a Jeep, which we could not unfortunately produce at that moment; much signing of autographs on both sides and nearly always the first question "What's your mob?" and finding several members of the Regiment in the camp, taken at Sidi Rezegh in 1941; and finally, on asking news of their erstwhile captors, being told that they were not long gone and were carrying panzerfausts. This was more serious, with all these fellows about, and on asking the police to clear the road we got the first startling proof of the state of the camp discipline. For at a word from a tall figure wearing the Airborne beret, RSM Lord, the

Tanks Advance! Lt Col (now Maj Gen) A R Leakey giving the orders over the radio to the 5th Royal Tank Regiment during the advance on Bremen.

Camp MP's went round, and in a very few moments and without a murmur these scores of men, some of whom were tasting freedom for the first time in more than five years, made their way back behind that same barbed wire and netting that to them must have been a symbol of all that was hateful and depressing of this life.

We left as the vanguard of visitors was arriving, the VIP's and the not so VIP's, the Press and the frankly curious, all wishing to to get a first-hand glimpse of the first large predominantly British camp to find itself in the path of the British Army of Liberation. And we left taking with us an impression that will never fade; of men whose courage and hope had been kept alive through long years of boredom and privation by their faith in their comrades and their country; and whose behaviour in their moment of triumph when faith had been rewarded was an example of the highest traditions of the Army to which they belonged.

And that might have been the end of our part in the proceedings of what was for all of us a great occasion. But later on that day we happened to pass that way again when things were more normal; erstwhile prisoners strolling about in groups, or sitting in the sun enjoying a smoke and waving contentedly at the passing traffic. But all was not quite normal, for as we came up to the main gates where we had received such a reception a few hours earlier, we saw a troop of armoured cars obliging some movie-cameramen by driving slowly past a group of wildly waving and shouting ex-prisoners; and for a brief moment, as we beheld the scene as spectators and not actors, we felt again all the emotions of that most memorable day.'

Surrender

Surrender. Brig John
Spurling entering Hamburg
Town Hall, May 3rd, 1945,
accompanied by Captains
Mitchell (GSO3) and
Lewisohn (IO) with
mapboard.
General Alwin Wolz,
Commander Hamburg
Garrison is saluting. The
smiling German officer
standing next to him is his
Intelligence Officer who
was educated at Oxford
University and is wearing a
Christchurch scarf. The
mayor is standing behind
in civilian clothes.

Above: Scout Cars of the Eleventh Hussars crossing the Elbe bridge into Hamburg.

Top right: Squadron Headquarters, D Sqn, 11th Hussars outside Hamburg Town Hall, May 3rd, 1945.

Centre, bottom right: Hamburg – The extent of the damage caused by months of air raids can be seen in these photos of the desolation in the streets of the city.

The Final Act

During late April 1945 it became very clear that the total defeat of Germany was not far off. Indeed, there were really only two outstanding questions to be answered – firstly, who was willing to surrender the German Armed Forces and secondly, would they obey a call to lay down their arms. The build up towards final capitulation on the 21st Army Group front began with minor local surrenders and parleys and ended with the negotiations for the surrender of Hamburg.

Throughout this confused period the commander of Hamburg Garrison, Major General Alwin Wolz, was wrestling with his conscience, trying to decide whether or not he should surrender the city. Certainly the influential and realistic members of the Hamburg Chamber of Commerce wanted it in order to prevent further destruction to their already much battered city. However, some elements of the German armed forces, still displaying fanatical devotion to the Fuhrer, were against it. Clearly General Wolz was afraid that he might become a scapegoat. Nevertheless he began secret negotiations. By May 1st his troubles were virtually over as General Keitel had ordered him to surrender on behalf of Admiral Doenitz. He was further told that a delegation of general

and admirals from the German High command would be arriving the following morning en route to see the British Army Group Commander. So, whilst General Wolz was agreeing at his level with GOC 7th Armoured Division to allow British troops to enter Hamburg, General Admiral von Friedeburg was leading a delegation to negotiate a complete surrender with Field Marshal Montgomery.

Let us start our examination of the final act at a slightly lower level with the thoughts of a young captain of the Eleventh Hussars, Richard Brett-Smith (as recorded in his book *Berlin '45*) as he waited with the leading British troops to enter Hamburg, the largest city ever to surrender to the British Army . . .

'We did not know, when we waited on our armoured cars that afternoon of May 3rd, 1945, ready to enter Hamburg, whether we would have to fight our way up Schleswig-Holstein and into Denmark, or not. Naturally we hoped that we would not have to, but we knew that our entry into Germany's second city and the events of the subsequent day would settle our doubts one way or the other.

We were supposed to lead in the 7th Armoured Division at three o'clock. It was a grey, depressing sort of day, and for some

reason we were held up. It started to rain, and for hours we waited in the drizzle, moving forward by slow degrees with an enormous and seemingly never-ending column behind us. Already a few tanks and some infantry had gone forward to secure the Elbe bridges, and a number of unauthorised explorers and joy-riders had penetrated into the city by design or by mistake.

At last, when it was nearly seven o'clock in the evening, we led the Division through Harburg and over the Elbe into Hamburg itself. Harburg had prepared us a little for what we were to see, but even so Hamburg was a terrible sight. Yet it was miraculously tidy. A few people lined the streets in quiet wonder, but there was hardly a sound as we passed through, except for the slight whine of our gears changing and the buzzing and whistling of our wireless sets. Scores of Hamburg policemen in their bright-green uniforms directed us on our way, most of them middle-aged or elderly men, for no-where did one see a young man not in the Wehrmacht, unless he was a cripple or a physical weakling.

There was something unnatural about the silence, something a little uncanny. As we drove up to that last great bridge across the Elbe, the final obstacle that could have held

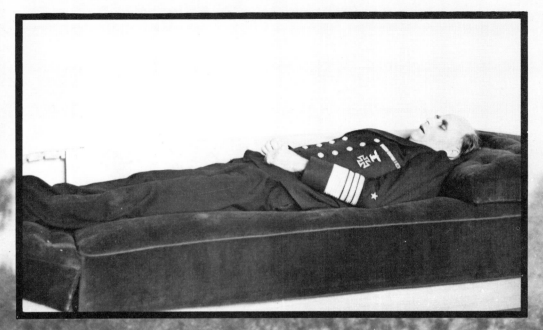

Above: The body of von Friedeburg. When he was told how the war situation was von Friedeburg burst into tears. He committed suicide shortly after the unconditional surrender had been signed.

Centre, bottom left: Admiral Hoffman arriving to surrender the German Navy on behalf of Gross Admiral Doenitz.

Right: The delegation arrives (L to R – Two Liaison Officers from HQ 21 Army Group, General-Admiral von Friedeburg, Capt Horsford 11H, German driver.

us up so long, it seemed impossible that we had taken Hamburg so easily. Looking down at the cold grey waters of the Elbe swirling far beneath, we sensed again that queer feeling that came whenever we crossed an enemy bridge, and it would have been no great surprise if the whole structure had suddenly collapsed and our cars plunged headlong into the river. But no, it did not blow up', and we found ourselves safely across, and so apparently did those behind us. Now at last we could heave a sigh of relief, for we were across the last obstacle, the Elbe, and there were no more rivers to cross, at worst only the Kiel Canal!'

Brett-Smith's Squadron made straight for the Atlantic Hotel on the shores of the Grosse Alster where until recently Himmler had had his headquarters. Meanwhile, in the centre of the city the surrender ceremony had taken place that afternoon in the Adolf Hitler Platz. Here General Wolz, together with his officers, had paraded to wait for the arrival of the 'British General'.

'But the General was denied the pomp and ceremony that he thought the occasion demanded. He and his officers had paraded in their smartest uniforms and full decorations in the otherwise deserted main square, to await the British General. But the first British vehicle to arrive had been a "water-bug" (15 cwt water truck) of the 7th Queens, which had flashed through the square, irrepressibly shabby and obviously miles off its route. Its unperturbed driver grinned at the Germans and shouted some ribald remarks at them. They stiffly ignored him.

The next arrival promised better. He was, in fact, our Colonel, in a Daimler scout car. The Germans sprang to attention, and

Below: A half track belonging to 3 RHA approaching the bridge over the Kiel Canal.

Right: After VE Day – Vehicles of D Squadron 11th Hussars in the main square of Tonning, a pleasant seaside town on the Eiderstadt Peninsula. Brigadier Spurling, Commander 131 Brigade, can be seen in the background going into the Military Goverment offices with a German officer.

Bottom right: Officers of D Sqn 11th Hussars receiving the surrender of a small German town.

General Wolz, a rather fat man with spectacles, advanced towards Colonel Wainman, whom he took to be the Divisional commander, figuratively waving the keys of Hamburg in his face. The Colonel, who was dressed in an American combat jacket and a pair of Bedford cords, climbed briskly out of his car, totally ignored the General, and walked over to the only other occupants of the square, some tame pigeons who lived there, whom he began to feed with Army biscuit.'

First Desert Rat into Hamburg
Although the Eleventh Hussars were the first unit to enter the city, the prize for being

the first British soldier to enter Hamburg officially must be given to a staff car driver from HQ 7th Armoured Division who, when General Wolz's own Mercedes broke down, was lent with his car to the Hamburg commander to return him to the Town Hall in time to prepare for the official entry ceremony. However, I have heard about an officer who claimed that he came into Hamburg from the Lauenburg direction early in the morning of the 3rd, believing that British troops were already in the town. He found the streets empty, apart from German police at every road junction who waved him forward, but no British troops. As the truth dawned on him he beat a hasty retreat!

The Surrender of the City Takes Place

'At 1800 hours on May 3rd, Brig Spurling, guided by Major Andrae and accompanied by Captains Mitchell and Hodson, reached the main entrance to Hamburg Rathaus. Here he was met by General Wolz, accompanied by Burgermeister Burchard-Motz and Hauptmann Dr Link as interpreter. General Wolz made formal transfer of the military command. The Brigadier was then conducted upstairs to the Burgermeistersaal. Here Gauleiter Kaufmann stood alone in the middle of the room, behind him a group of senators and members of the party. Brigadier and gauleiter greeted each other and walked to a table in the corner of the room. As a matter of history it was round that table that the act of civil surrender took place. Brigadier Spurling, as civil administrator until a military governor should take over, charged the German officials present to be responsible to him for law and order in the city. It was nearly seven o'clock on the evening of May 3rd. The surrender of Hamburg had taken place.

These weighty matters having been settled, Gauleiter Kaufmann told Brigadier Spurling that he, the gauleiter, had already arranged

for the British commander and his staff to be accommodated at the nearby Atlantic Hotel, where they would find dinner prepared for them. Such was in fact the case. Major Morrison, the leading Military Government officer, had meanwhile reached Hamburg and was discussing detailed matters of administration with Rathaus officials. Later that evening, the commander and staff of 8 Base Sub-Area came into the city and lodged in the "Vier Jahreszeiten' (The Four Seasons Hotel). They had come straight up from Ostend and were charged with the vitally important task of opening up the port of Hamburg.

General Lyne himself established his caravan headquarters on the evening of May 3rd on the shores of the Aussen Alster. This was, however, an overnight stop; he and his division were destined to move further north into Schleswig-Holstein. It is General Lyne's testimony to General Wolz's efficient telephone communications and the discipline of his anti-aircraft division that not one single shot was fired at the British troops as they moved into the city, nor was there any breakdown in command. The population remained in their houses. No white flags

were visible anywhere. For Hamburg the war was over. The rest is the story of Military Government.' (Taken from *The Capitulation of Hamburg 3rd May 1945* by Dr J K Dunlop published in the RUSI Journal February 1954.)

Another young captain of the Eleventh Hussars who also witnessed these eventful happenings was Richard Moore. Shortly afterwards he wrote the following letter home:

'Dear Mother,
We do live in stirring times. The events of the last two days from our angle will interest you.

After some days of the Hamburg negotiations and standing by for more all the time; finally after delays and hitches, "on a much, much higher level" as they say on the wireless, in we went. Then yesterday after a night spent in a bank, of all places (no money but primuses on the counter brewing up!) and the Moffer (German soldiers) coming by in their hundreds, a message to expect a big cheese and later on other messages to me on the rear link to alert people to meet the big

The End of the German Army. Some of the thousands of German soldiers, men of every conceivable age and unit who jostled one another in complete disorder as they came to give themselves up. Some could hardly walk and plodded along with the aid of sticks, their arms long since thrown away. The motley collection of vehicles they had collected towed each other along (the record seen by the 11th Hussars was eight cars being pulled by one lorry!)

Right: Men of the
Eleventh Hussars show off a
captured Swastika.

Below: 'D' Squadron
Eleventh Hussars' Bonfire on
VE-Day May 8th, 1945. 'That
wonderful night will never
be forgotten by anyone who
was there with hordes of
strange fur-coated figures
swigging rum punch and
singing their hearts out.
Verey lights ricochetting all
over the place and the
Colonel going round each
squadron in turn, and each
squadron striving to produce
a bigger and better 'brew-up'
for him than the last and
succeeding only too well'[1]

(1) 'The Eleventh at War'
p.479.

Bottom: Vehicles of Tac
Divisional HQ near the
shores of the Aussen Alster
in Hamburg. The houses
they occupied temporarily
had been vacated by the
Gestapo.

cheese. By and by up came our people and
we all (SHQ and the representatives from 21st
Army Group) went up to the leading troop
on the road to Kiel.

By now the Moffer were coming past in
their thousands, lorries, carts, bicycles, buses
and everything, but mainly walking not
marching and looking unbelievably lost,
every vestige of discipline and smartness
gone. There, we with the colonels waited –
the classic scene being an MP looting some
eggs, he in immaculate redcap, the whitest of
belts and shiniest of boots and us in fur coats,
corduroys and God knows what, all eating
fried eggs and drinking char.

Finally along came Admiral Freideberg to
negotiate the surrender, as you know, in a
car by himself and soon after a Wehrmacht
staff officer in another; the cameras clicked
and they talked for a few minutes. I thought
Toby was going to loot the admiral's car, he
was chatting away to him and looking into it!
Then off they went and we settled down to
the business of raking in and organising
several thousand POW, the local police and
so on, including several hundred Russian,
Polish, French and God knows what else, in
ancient vehicles of all sorts, mostly run on
wood and coal and *all* on tow, off to a camp
one of the other squadrons is running, and so
on again until after midnight and early next
morning (today) again still as thick as ever.
More big cheeses from the other side,
including two who came in and more or less

offered us the Luftwaffe and later on Admiral Hoffman from Doenitz who wanted to get rid of the Fleet. They all came along and asked for Field Marshal Montgomery most correctly – get shown in to Toby and me who usually give them tea and/or cognac and pass them on. The reaction from asking for the Field Marshal and getting two buckshees, in pretty rough kit, is worth seeing. Next the BBC, Vaughan Williams or some one arrived to see the Moffer coming in; so they had tea and cognac, then went up to Reggie and did a recording. The real highlight of the day was Tom Suggitt, the signal sergeant, with a news flash from the BBC – "Huddersfield has won the Rugby Cup" and as an afterthought later on "two Moffer armies have surrendered somewhere!"

Unconditional Surrender

The delegation under General Admiral von Freideburg signed a document of unconditional surrender at 1820 hours on May 4th, 1945. This related only to the forces in Holland, the Fresian Islands, Heligoland, Schleswig Holstein and Denmark who were facing 21st Army Group. It was not until May 6th that the final unconditional surrender of all Land, Sea and Air Forces of the Third Reich was made.

It is fitting that we should close this chapter with the Special Order of the Day issued by the GOC 7th Armoured Division:

SPECIAL ORDER OF THE DAY
by
Major General L O LYNE CB, DSO
Commander, 7 Armoured Division

(To be read out to all troops on parade)

The war with Germany is won. It has ended with the complete and final defeat and destruction of the German Armed Forces.

No Division in the British Empire has contributed more to this result than the 7th Armoured Division.

Through the long years of fighting in the Middle East, in Tunisia, in Italy and throughout the campaign in North West Europe, our Division has always been in the thick of it.

Your rapid advance from the Rhine to the Elbe, and the hard fighting which made this possible, contributed very greatly to the brilliant success of the whole campaign.

I wish to congratulate every officer and man in the Division upon their fine achievements, and to thank them personally for their loyalty and unflagging enthusiasm.

Difficult days may lie ahead of us in the transition period from war to peace, but you will overcome these as you have overcome all difficulties in the past.

It will be a great honour in the future to be able to say "I was a Desert Rat".

Main Headquarters,
7 British Armoured Division
7 May 45

L. O. LYNE
Major-General
Commander

Above centre: Victory
Parade. Vehicles of the
Division moving towards
the saluting base.

Berlin~The Greatest Day

On June 14th, 1945, whilst the Division was busy settling down to the job of occupational duties north of Hamburg, orders came from 21 Army Group that the Desert Rats must stand by to move to Berlin. Unfortunately it was impossible to take the whole Division due to lack of accommodation there, and so on June 16th orders were issued that the following units would stand by at 48 hours notice to move:

Tactical Divisional Headquarters
Headquarters 131 Infantry Brigade
3rd Royal Horse Artillery
8th Hussars
11th Hussars
1st/5th Queens
2nd Devons
4th Field, 621st Field and 143rd Field Park Squadrons, Royal Engineers.

In addition, in order to make the force as fully representative as possible 21 Army Group placed under command 1st Battalion Grenadier Guards from the Guards Armoured Division and a composite Canadian Battalion from the 1st Canadian Army. One can imagine how much excitement the prospect of the move created. Here is how Sergeant Joseph Lodge of 2nd Devons remembers it: 'When we first heard of our move to Berlin I think every man from private soldier to officer were so elated that it would be really impossible to describe or even guess at each man's thoughts. I know for myself and the

MONS TO BERLIN

"Well, the boys have got there at last."

forty or fifty men nearest to me we looked upon it as a great honour to think we were to be stationed in the very heart of Germany. The actual move I do not remember all that much about. I know that it was a very slow process what with the large numbers of troops and vehicles involved, also the bloody-mindedness of the Russians when it came to entering their sector. When we did eventually reach our destination (Spandau Barracks) we thought that under the very difficult circumstances they met, our advance party had done a good job.

The first few weeks were spent cleaning up and trying to make life a little more pleasant. The non-fraternisation with the German population came very hard to us all, seeing the utter destruction of Berlin one had to have just a little feeling of pity for the civilian population and, as everybody knows, the hardest thing for a British soldier once he comes in contact with anybody is not to be friendly. Our Brigadier visited us after a very short time, a really bull parade – all went well until our company was ready for inspection, eyes front, was given in turn by all platoon sergeants. Support Company (mine) was head of the parade, I gave the final eyes front and then instead of stepping off I froze to the spot – got a bit of a ripping from the RSM it had been a terrible night in the Mess the night before as I'm sure all 2nd Devon sergeants will remember!

After a while everybody seemed to get themselves organised, what we would now explain as "doing their own thing". Some took up football, horseriding, many went on different courses, I think more for a rest than anything. I went on an anti-tank course in which funnily I had specialised for the last two years of the war – no change but very enjoyable.'

The main body of the Division arrived on July 4th, which began with a deluge of rain but fortunately cleared up later. Led by 'C' Squadron 11th Hussars, the Division reached the saluting base on Pichelsdorfer Strasse about half past six that evening, where the GOC was waiting to greet them. There followed a period of intense activity cleaning and repairing their accommodation and rehearsing for the many ceremonial parades which took place over the next few days.

The first of these was on July 6th when the Union Jack was hoisted on the biggest flagpole which could be found, at the foot of the Franco-Prussian War Memorial in the Grosse Stern. The GOC had charged the commander of 131 Brigade, Brigadier (now Major General) John Spurling, with the task of finding the flagpole and his resourceful sapper field squadron commander decided to 'borrow' one from the Olympic Stadium, some four miles away. Transportation proved a problem and eventually the Berlin Fire Brigade had to be called in to help move the enormous pole. The sappers then set to work making a hole in the pavement to set in the pole. They were so busy getting it erected and concreting it into the floor of a conveniently

Far left, top: Mons to Berlin. 'Well the boys have got here at last' (E H Shepherd drawing from Punch, July 11th, 1945 and reproduced here by kind permission of the proprietors).

Far left, bottom: The last leg. Vehicles of the Division on the autobahn en route for Berlin from Helmstedt.

Centre bottom: Passing Russian troops on the autobahn en route for Berlin from Helmstedt.

Below: Magdeburg Bridge. On July 1st, 1945 the Div Recce party started to cross the Elbe by the autobahn bridge built by the Russians alongside this one which had been blown. The GOC was leading the column and after the first few vehicles had crossed a Russian sentry appeared on the far side and said that his orders were to allow no vehicles of any type or nationality over and that all traffic should use the temporary 'Friendship' bridge in Magdeburg. Arguments and persuasion by the GOC proved to no avail and the column had to turn around and use the other bridge.

placed underground public loo, that they forgot to paint it. Resourceful to the end, however, Brigadier John Spurling obtained the services of a Japanese acrobat from the Hamburg Circus, to shin up the pole with a pot of paint! The same acrobat was required to perform again later that day when the French decided they wanted the Tricolour flying on top of the Franco-Prussian War Memorial.

The Greatest Day

Finally the greatest day of all arrived and at 10 o'clock on the morning of July 21st, 1945, a roar of guns broke out over the ruins of Berlin, as the 3rd Regiment Royal Horse Artillery fired a 19 gun salute in honour of the Right Honorable Winston Churchill who was to take the salute at the Victory Parade.

The programme of events for the Parade was as follows:

1000 hours – The Prime Minister accompanied by the Commander-in-Chief arrives at the Saluting Base. Met by GOC British Troops, Berlin. Salute by guns of 3RHA.

1005 hours – The Prime Minister, accompanied by Distinguished Visitors, drives round and inspects the Parade.

1030 hours – The Prime Minister returns to the Saluting Base.

1035 hours – March Past begins.

1110 hours – March Past ends.

1115 hours – The Prime Minister departs.

As the guns, tanks, armoured cars and carriers thundered past the saluting base, followed by the marching troops, the feelings of all those taking part in this great cavalcade would have been well worth recording. One can only speculate, however, as did General Verney in his history of the Division:

'What thoughts must have passed through the minds of the veterans as they saluted their great war leader! Of that first venture through the wire of the Egyptian frontier and the overwhelming victory of Beda Fomm and Sidi Saleh; of Sidi Rezegh in November 1941; and the desperate fighting in that same area a few months later; Alam Halfa and Alamein; Tripoli and Tunis; the crossing of the Volturno; the bloody fighting in the Bocage and the Plains of Caen; the exhilarating scenes of "Liberation" on the long road to Ghent; the harsh winter battles and the last long advance into the heart of the enemy's country.

So many scenes, good times and bad, savage heat and extreme cold, sand storms and snow, rain and sunshine and perhaps, too, so many names – O'Connor and Creagh the first architects of victory: Gott and Campbell; Pinney, Ward Gunn and Beeley; Holliman and Wainman and all those others whose names find no written records but who gave their whole endeavours to their comrades and their Regiments, who died in battle or afterwards, who will be honoured and remembered for all time by those who served with them' (*The Desert Rats, North Africa*, page 282.)

Top left: Poster on the road into Berlin.

Top centre: Berlin at last! Tanks of the Division entering Berlin July 4th, 1945.

Above: The GOC taking the salute in the Pichelsdorfer Strasse as the Division enters Berlin 1825 hours, July 4th, 1945. (Nobody seems to have noticed that the Union Jack was upside down).

Left: The entrance to the Reich Chancellery in the Wilhelmstrasse. The balcony on the right of the building was used by Hitler for making speeches and reviewing troops. (Note also the two Russian guards).

143

This series of photographs was taken by Major Christopher Milner of the Rifle Brigade using a 'looted' film which had been used before to photograph prisoners in Dulag XIB, hence the ghostly background faces

Above: Berlin 1945. The Brandenburg Tor.

Top right: Berlin 1945. Fuel shortage. Note the World War I British tank in the background.

Far right: Berlin 1945. The Brandenburg Tor, note the Red Flag draped over the statue.

Right: Inside the devastated Reich Chancellery which had been looted and disfigured with graffiti in Russian and English.

'*Dear Desert Rats*'

Memorable though the parade undoubtedly was, to my mind it was the moving eloquence of Churchill which really set the seal on this the greatest of days. After the parade, whilst opening the 'Winston' Club he said: 'Soldiers of the 7th Armoured Division. I am delighted to be able to open this Club and I shall always consider it a great honour that it should have been named after me.

I have, not for the first time, had the pleasure of seeing your troops march past, and this brings back to my mind a great many moving incidents in these last, long, fierce years.

Now, here in Berlin, I find you all established in this great centre, from which, as from a volcano, fire and smoke and poison fumes have erupted all over Europe twice in a generation. And in bygone times also German fury has been let loose on her neighbours, and now it is we who have our place in the occupation of this country.

I feel I can go so far as to ask Field Marshal Montgomery to signalise this happy event of the great Victory Parade we have had today

DUL XI B

200100

200099

DUL XI B

200097

XI B

200096

by giving a whole holiday to all the troops in Berlin, and I hope, Field Marshal, that you can accommodate this to operational and other necessities.

Now I have only a word more to say about the Desert Rats. They were the first to begin. The 11th Hussars were in action in the desert in 1940 and ever since you have kept marching steadily forward on the long road to victory. Through so many countries and changing scenes you have fought your way.

It is not without emotion that I can express to you what I feel about the Desert Rats.

Dear Desert Rats! May your glory ever shine! May your laurels never fade! May the memory of this glorious pilgrimage of war which you have made from Alamein, via the Baltic to Berlin, never die! It is a march unsurpassed through all the story of war so far as my reading of history leads me to believe. May the fathers long tell the children about this tale. May you all feel that in following your great ancestors you have accomplished something which has done good to the whole world; which has raised the honour of your own country and which every man has a right to be proud of'. (Extract from *A Short History of the 7th Armoured Division June 1943–July 1945*.)

Top left: Berlin 1945. Old armoured car.

Above: Berlin 1945. Russian soldiers using horse drawn transport.

Left, far left: Bomb damage in Berlin 1945. The capital of the Third Reich had been devastated by bombs and weapons of all types before suffering the crowning indignity of being occupied by enemy forces.

Above: Berlin 1945. The Russians erected enormous copies of photographs of the Allied War leaders on the Unter den Linden.

Centre left: Berlin 1945. More Russian photographs, these are of some of their top generals in the Alexander Platz.

Bottom left: Berlin 1945. The Black Market flourished in the Tiergarten in front of the gutted Reichstag.

Top right: Hoisting the Union Jack at the foot of the Franco-Prussian War Memorial in the Grosse Stern, July 6th, 1945.

Right: Hand-over of French Sector. Brig John Spurling together with his French opposite number inspects the Guard of Honour of the Eleventh Hussars.

BRITISH VICTORY PARADE

BERLIN

21ˢᵀ JULY 1945

Above centre: Victory Parade. Vehicles of the Division moving towards the saluting base.

Above left: Hand-over of French Sector. Flag ceremony in progress.

Left: Cover of the programme for the British Victory Parade, July 21st, 1945.

Top right: The 3rd Regiment Royal Horse Artillery firing a nineteen gun salute in honour of the Prime Minister, the Right Honourable Winston Churchill's arrival to take the Victory Parade.

Right: Victory Parade. A scene at the Saluting base showing Mr Winston Churchill, Fd Marshal Sir Harold Alexander, Fd Marshal Sir Bernard Montgomery, Mr Anthony Eden and Mr Clement Attlee, together with GOC 7th Armoured Division, Gen 'Lou' Lyne.

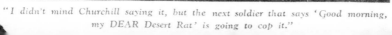
"I didn't mind Churchill saying it, but the next soldier that says 'Good morning, my DEAR Desert Rat' is going to cop it."

Left: Victory Parade. The Inspection in progress. Mr Churchill, together with other VIPs in a half track, moves slowly past tanks of the Division.

Right: Victory Parade. The Colour Party of the 2nd Battalion, The Devonshire Regiment marching towards the saluting base.

Bottom left: Dear Desert Rats. As usual Giles manages to catch the humour of the moment in this cartoon which appeared in the 'Daily Express' on July 24th, 1945 and is reproduced here with his kind permission.

Bottom centre: Opening the 'Winston' Club. After the parade, Mr Churchill opened the 'Winston' Club, making his famous 'Dear Desert Rats' speech, part of which is reproduced at the end of this section.

Bottom right: Opening the Jerboa Club. Major General 'Lou' Lyne cutting the tape at the entrance to the Desert Rats new club in Berlin July 23rd, 1945.

'Roll on my Demob'

PERSONAL MESSAGE
from
COMMANDER
7th ARMOURED DIVISION
to
EVERY OFFICER AND MAN
ON DEMOBILISATION

•

MAIN HEADQUARTERS
7th ARMOURED DIVISION

You may well be very proud to have served with the 7th Armoured Division. No Division in the British Empire has contributed more to the downfall of the Axis Powers and to the total defeat of Germany.

The Desert Rats first saw service in the Middle East, when Italy declared war on us in 1940. They fought with great distinction all through the long campaign which culminated in the victory of ALAMEIN. They took a leading part in the pursuit of Rommel's defeated forces, and in the final breakthrough to TUNIS.

The Division was the first British Armoured Division to land in Europe, when it took part in the assault landing at SALERNO. It served through the Italian Campaign till brought back to England early in 1944 to prepare for the great assault on Western Europe.

Once more the Division formed part of an assault Corps and fought hard throughout Normandy and the winter campaign. Finally, the 7th Armoured Division crossed the RHINE and made history by its rapid advance to the ELBE and subsequent occupation of HAMBURG.

This is a grand and glorious record. The credit for it belongs to you, to each individual officer and man.

I think that there are three particular qualities to which we can ascribe our success:

(1) THE FIRM BELIEF WHICH WE HAVE HELD IN THE IDEALS FOR WHICH WE HAVE FOUGHT, THE RESTORATION OF CHRISTIAN CIVILISATION TO THE WORLD; AND OUR TRUST IN GOD TO GIVE US THE POWER TO ACHIEVE THIS.

(2) OUR FIGHTING SPIRIT AND THE DETERMINATION TO OVERCOME ALL DIFFICULTIES,

(3) OUR TEAM SPIRIT AND THE DESIRE THAT ALL WE ACHIEVE MAY BE FOR THE COMMON END AND NOT FOR SELFISH GAIN.

These three great guiding motives have stood out like shining beacons, not to us alone, but to all men and women of the United Nations.

We have won the war; now for the peace.

Difficult times and hard work for all of us lie ahead if we are to restore the ravages of five-and-a-half years of war. The same sterling qualities which led our country through every peril to final victory will help us again.

I hope that you will carry back to civilian life with you those three fine qualities which have played so predominant a part in the life of this Division. I am sure that if you do we shall win the peace as completely as we have won the war.

Finally, I wish to thank you for all that you have done for the Division, and to wish you happiness and good fortune in the years to come.

L. O. Lyne

Major-General,
Commander,
7th Armoured Division.

Roll on My Demob!

The road to Civvy Street and a good job was not always easy for the returning Desert Rat as is evidenced by this cautionary tale entitled 'Post War Plans' which appeared in the second issue of the 'Jerboa Geordie' published on November 15th, 1945. This was the fortnightly journal of No 3 Independent Machine Gun Company, Royal Northumberland Fusiliers, who were part of 131 Brigade throughout the North West European campaign:

'I was half way through my leave – the last one I would have in the Army – sprawled comfortably in my favourite chair, in front of a roaring fire, and feeling thoroughly at peace with the world.

Two months to go, I thought, and then I'll be a fully-fledged civvy. After six years of blood and tears, good times and bad, I'd be free once more to do as I liked. What would I do? Well, first of all there was that fortnight's holiday I had promised to have with my wife – we hadn't had a decent one during the war – then get a job and settle down.

A job! The thought brought me back to earth with a jolt. My old job had been blitzed, and anyway, I wanted something better, now that I was a family man. The more I thought of it, the more I realised that now was the time to find a job, while I had plenty of time to spare. Suiting the action to the word, I picked up the evening paper once more, and scanned the "Situations Vacant" column. There was quite a selection to choose from, and I couldn't decide which one to apply for, so I thought the best idea was to try a few of them in person in the morning.

Next morning at 0830 hours I was all dressed and ready for the fray, much to the surprise of my wife. "Where do you think you're going at this hour?" she asked. "Looking for a job" I replied. "No good waiting until I'm demobbed; strike while the iron's hot. Do It Now – that's my motto from now on".

My first port of call was a gent's outfitters – I always did fancy myself as a seller of fancy socks. Meekly I asked for the manager, and as a huge man advanced and towered over me, my knees turned to water.

"Well what can I do for you?" he rumbled. "I've come about that job you advertised in the News last night" I squeaked. "Any references?" he growled. "No, I've been six years in the Army though". "What did you do in the Army?" Here is my chance I thought, and proudly swelling my chest to its glorious $28\frac{1}{2}$ inches I said "I was a driver/operator".

"Um, I've heard of them" he said in a pitiful sort of voice, "No good for anything that requires hard work. No resistance – nothing. Better try somewhere else. Good morning".

Dejectedly, I looked at the next name on the list – Smithers, grocers in High Street. Surely I could weigh a pound of sugar! Boldly I marched in and asked for the boss. This man was short and thin, and going bald on top, and had an expression of constant worry on his face. In the advanced stages of couponitis I thought, so he should be easy to handle. Going straight into the attack I said "I'm looking for a job, and thought the position which you advertised last night would just suit me. I've been six years in the Army, and rose to the rank of corporal." "So did Hitler" he barked, "And look what a mess he made of his firm. No, I

couldn't take the risk. Good day". Blindly I stumbled out on to the pavement, and realising that they had just opened, I decided to have a tonic.

Looking at my list, I found my next chance lay with S. Windle & Co., jewellers. Just in my line, selling watches and rings was the easiest thing in the world, or so it seemed as I watched the transactions in Berlin. I opened the shop door and walked in, and immediately an oily individual oozed towards me, rubbing his greasy palms together. "Vat can I get der chentlmans?" he blubbered, in a voice which made me feel bilious. "You advertised last night for an assistant and I'm just the man you want". "Vat other jobs have you did" he wheezed. "Guard commander, i/c reliefs, and orderly corporal, so you will see that I'm a man of great initiative and highest integrity. Why, many's the time the Sergeant-Major has left me in complete charge of a brand new order board".

"Vat part of Chermany did you occupy?" asked the oily one. "Berlin", I answered proudly. "Ah! You are a Rat! The chap I just sacked vos also a Rat, he took seven watches and left twenty fags in der till. Once a Rat, always a Rat!"

This was too much for me, and I slammed the door behind me and I tramped home, deciding that as soon as I got back to Berlin, I would sign on – maybe they can make me permanent company runner!' (Reproduced by kind permission of RHQ (Northumberland) The Royal Regiment of Fusiliers; Journal loaned by R. Jarvie Esq.)

Far left: This card was given to all ranks of the Division on demobilisation.

Below: Cartoon reproduced by kind permission of Jon.

"Don't worry old man, Pte. Blenkinsop assured me he'd fix us up with a job"

Sand at the Finish

Sand at the Finish

'The General had already made his farewell speech to the men; a fatigue party had been detailed to take down the headquarters signboard and the guard commander had been instructed to lower the Divisional flag for the last time.

In the Sergeant's Mess at 7th Armoured Division headquarters, RSM Jack Allen, who had joined the Division in the desert as a tank commander in 1941, raised his glass and called for a last toast: "Gentlemen, here's to 7th Armoured Division – the finest in the British Army".

Sergeant Albert Saunders unhooked a fire

Maj General 'Pip Roberts, GOC in 1948, toasting his Desert Rats at the first disbandment of the Division at Bad Rothenfelde.

bucket from the wall, took out a handful of sand and spread it at the feet of his comrades. It was a sentimental but fitting last gesture from one of the original Desert Rats to the memory of a division which has now been disbanded, but which will live long in the memories of all who proudly wore the famous Jerboa sign'. (Quoted from *Soldier* Magazine, March 1948).

That is how E J Grove, a reporter for *Soldier* magazine described the scene in 1948 at the first disbandment of the Division when Major General Pip Roberts, CB, DSO, MC, was commanding and Divisional Headquarters was located in the Westphalian village of Bad Rothenfelde. General Pip had been in command since January 1946 and had guided the Division through the difficult period of occupational duties. He had commanded 11th Armoured Division in the latter stages of the war, but was no stranger to 7th Armoured, having been a Desert Rat for most of the North African campaign, his last appointment with the Division being as Commander of 22nd Armoured Brigade at the time of the capture of Tripoli. He was described in an Army Quarterly of the day as "the living embodiment of all that has been best in the Division". In his farewell message to his Desert Rats he expressed the hope that the Division would be reformed and fortunately his words proved to be prophetic. About the time of the Berlin airlift and the beginning of the Cold War, the Division was reformed and went on to serve with distinction for a further period in the British Army of the Rhine, until it was once again disbanded on April 16th, 1958. On this occasion the Division was redesignated as '5th Division', which under a year later was yet again re-designated as '1st Division'.

The Times leader, published on the day following the disbandment parade, was a mark of the high esteem in which the Desert Rats were held:

'The glories of the British Army are by tradition enshrined in the permanent regiments and corps which go to make it up. Divisions and brigades, being essentially ephemeral formations, have not so often caught the public imagination, though there are exceptions to this rule dating back to the Light Division in the Peninsula, and the Light Brigade in the Crimea. The First World War served to build up a number of divisional reputations. In the second several divisions acquired a name first within the Army and then throughout the nation for consistent valour and prowess in different theatres of war. But it is no exaggeration to say that the 7th Armoured Division, the Desert Rats, won more renown than any division has ever gained in the history of the British Army. There are those who felt, and feel today, that this was unfair. There are other divisions which won equally glorious victories, endured equal butcheries and fought in even worse physical conditions.

Why then did the renown of the Desert Rats grow so mightily? One reason is that they were "first in and last out" of the battle. It is true that they did not fight at Dunkirk, but they were on active operations in the Western Desert from the beginning of the war, and as the only armoured division acquired a reputation in the Army equivalent to that of "the Few" in the RAF. Then there was the spectacular nature of some of their victories, the great distances covered, the masses of prisoners, and the restoration of speed to war. The news of these exploits served to hearten the Commonwealth at a time when there was not much else to be cheerful about. And they were sloggers too. At Sidi Rezegh, Knightsbridge and Alam Halfa they took fearful punishment.

The Desert Rats preserved a shining spirit. Rightly or wrongly, the concept of chivalry was retained among them in the circumstances of modern war. They were a light-hearted and happy division. Sir Winston Churchill in his memoirs recounts how, listening in London to a relay of one of the early desert battles, he heard with delight a squadron leader report "I am now at the second B in Buq Buq". They exemplified the attitude of the British to war at its most dangerous, which found a response among the British people. Some of their fame they undoubtedly owe to the inspired choice of an emblem by one of their earlier commanders, Major General Sir M O'Moore Creagh. Public relations are important, in war as in anything else. The nickname of the Desert Rats caught on. It is a lesson which the unimaginative generals who had decreed the end of this famous fighting force should take to heart.' (Published by kind permission of the *Times* Newspapers Limited.)

Third Time Unlucky?

But of course that was not the end of the story. You can't keep a good Rat down and the Jerboa went on being proudly worn by the men of the 7th Armoured Brigade who remain as the only formation with the Desert Rat emblem. Alas the demise of that tough little rodent which had been put off twice is now yet again a distinct possibility. It is fitting therefore that the present 'Chief Rat', Brigadier Martin Farndale, should have the last word:

'The Desert Rats live on in the name of 7th Armoured Brigade in Soltau, Germany. All the "Rat" property, silver, pictures and relics are there and annually the Brigade celebrates the battle of Sidi Rezegh on November 22nd. On that day a church service is held followed by a march past of the present generation of "Rats". The original battered flag of the desert days lies on the altar at the service and old comrades come out from England. It is a moving experience and serves as a reminder to each generation as it comes along, that the standards and example set in battle are not forgotten.

The Brigade in 1975 consists of two armoured regiments, 1st The Queen's Dragoon Guards and the 13th/18th Royal Hussars (Queen Mary's Own) and two mechanised infantry battalions, the 1st Battalion The King's Own Royal Border Regiment and the 1st Battalion The Prince of Wales's Own Regiment of Yorkshire. It is interesting to note that the Brigade's affiliated Squadron in the Royal Air Force, 20 Squadron (Harriers), proudly wears the Rat on the tails of its aircraft.

But alas are they to be the last custodians of the Rat? The Defence White Paper of March 1975 announced that Brigades are to be no more. Will the Rat go from the order of battle of the British Army? At the time of writing we do not know, but we do know that the Rat will never ever be forgotten. The fame of the Desert Rats has spread around the world, their exploits have never been equalled even by the marches of the Romans, Hannibal, Alexander the Great or Napoleon. No force in history has marched so far or fought so long. The Red Rat marched from Alamein to Naples and on to Berlin via Normandy while the Green Rat marched from India to Rangoon and always he marched to victory. Whatever happens the Rat will remain one of the greatest formation symbols of all time, the envy of all. Since the end of the war he has been in Germany demanding high standards from all who serve him and he remains now as bright, shiny and agile as he was when he was born in the desert of North Africa in 1941. Like the true old soldier that he is he will never die'.

Stand Down

Stand Down

Here are we met upon this day
To toast the golden past away,
To hand a duty gladly done
To those whose task has just begun.
We who have taken for our charm
The Desert Rat upon our arm,
Extend our greetings firm and true,
Ring out the old – ring in the new.

And now to King of all the Rats,
Those present here take off their hats;
A welcome then to General Lyne
The leader of our desert sign
Our toast before dividing ways:
'God send him happy all his days'.

So many here, so much to say,
So many dreams to dream away.
Memory cool and crystal clear
Lives on in every moment here.
Those days – those days! We're looking back!
Down a well worn Axis track.
Cairo, Knightsbridge, Alamein,
That never changing desert scene.

The scorching sun, the midnight stars,
Those ever stretching lonely hours.
The desert stove – the desert rose!
The secrets that the desert knows.
Always the desert, desert sand,
That hellish never never land.
But there was forged this bond so true
Which lives in everyone of you.

Then over blue and summer sea
To fight again in Italy.
To England after four long years,
Wisbech girls and Norwich beers.
So the months ran swiftly by
To bring the Rat to Normandy.

Bursting through across the Seine
We chased the bloody Bosche again.
That Belgian welcome felt we all
Could never be beyond recall.

Holland! Flat with cold and damp
Bogged us down with winter cramp.
And then the spring on winter's heels
Dried the mud and loosed our wheels.
At last the greatest show was near,
The Rhine was crossed, the future clear.

So in this land of evil fame
We say goodbye, but always claim
That he who marched so in this war
Has done a deed ne'er done before.
Proudly we share this brotherhood
By strangers scarcely understood.

And those who now do stand by me
Stand thus until eternity.
Long may their spirit breathe and live
Good Speed you – Seventh Armoured Div!

Taken from the menu of the 'Hail and Fare-well' dinner which was held in the Warrant Officers' and Sergeants' Mess, Headquarters, Seventh Armoured Division on November 7th, 1945.

Below: This splendid authentic bronze statue of a Jerboa was made by Brig George Davy, who commanded 7th Armoured Brigade at the Battle of Sidi Rezegh in November 1941. (His painting of the battle appears in the North African volume of this series).

Right: The End of the Road – The Divisional Axis board erected in Berlin in July 1945.

Bibliography

Books

Brett-Smith, Richard: *Berlin '45 The Grey City*, (Macmillan).

Chamberlain, Peter and Ellis, Chris: *Profile, AFV Weapons No 48*, (Profile Publications Ltd).

Clark, Dudley: *The Eleventh at War*, (Michael Joseph).

Evans, Roger: *The Story of the Fifth Royal Inniskilling Dragoon Guards*, (Gale & Polden).

Garnet, Jack (Editor): *Wardrop of the Fifth*, (Private).

Hastings, R.H.W.S.: *The Rifle Brigade in the Second World War 1939-1945*, (Gale & Polden).

Lindsay M. & Johnston H.E.: *The History of the 7th Armoured Division June 1943 – July 1945*, (Printing and Stationery Services, British Army of the Rhine).

Verney, G.L.: *The Desert Rats*, (Hutchinson).

Periodicals

Jerboa Geordie, November 15, 1948

RUSI Journal, February 1954

Soldier Magazine, March 1948

The Times, April 16, 1958

The Illustrated London News, various editions, 1944-45

Photo Credits

Maj J Alpe: 10, 16 (B), 20, 138, 141 (R), 144 (B), 149 (T), 150 (TR).

A Atkins: 15, 21 (Inset), 22 (T), 77, 78 (T), 137, 150 (B), 152 (B), 154, 155.

Maj A H Barnes: 14 (C), 16 (T), 42, 44, 48, 49 (B), 54, 54 (Inset), 55 (Inset), 56 (B), 58 (AC), 59 (B), 64 (T), 107 (T), 108 (TR), 108 (B).

F Black: 132 (B).

N Bloomfield: 40 (TL)

Mrs J Boggie: 103 (T), 108 (TL)

Maj Gen B H W Brind: 150 (TL), 153 (T)

S A Busby: 142 (TL)

Brig M L Crosthwait: 38 (C)

T P Dalton: 13

C Davis: 103 (C)

D Dickson: 52, 68, 69 (Inset), 70, 71, 72, 73, 98, 99 (B), 104 (T), 104 (B), 106 (L), 106 (TR), 110

Maj P N Erskine: 19 (T), 46 (B), 47

G Forty: 81

Maj I Fowler: 6

F Fromont: 79, 83 (Inset)

N Hall: 12, 58 (BC), 58 (B), 63 (C), 108 (C), 109, 111 (Inset)

R Hardy: 136 (T)

Rev E G Hazleton: 57 (T)

Home HQ 1 The Royal Hussars: 18

Illustrated London News: 62 (T), 66, 92, 94 (T), 122

Imperial War Museum: 2, 4, 8, 17, 26, 28, 30, 31, 32, 33, 35 (Inset), 36 (T), 37, 38 (T), 39, 40 (BR), 45, 46 (T), 56 (T), 57 (B), 60, 62 (B), 63 (T), 65, 67, 74, 76, 80, 88, 93, 94 (B), 95, 112, 116, 117, 118, 119, 120, 120 (Inset), 123, 124, 125, 126, 130 (T), 143 (T), 151 (T), 151 (B), 152 (T), 152 (BR), 153 (B)

Powell Jones: 63 (B)

J Kinsella: 103 (B)

Brig G S Knox: 105, 107 (B)

M H Leese: 129 (C), 129 (B)

H Martin: 50, 58 (T)

Mrs M Milburn: 110 (Inset)

Maj C Milner: 59 (T), 82, 84, 96, 99 (T), 101 (Inset), 140 (B), 140 (BR), 144 (T), 145, 146 (T), 148 (B)

Mrs S M Moore: 59 (C), 128, 129 (T), 130 (C), 130 (B), 131, 133, 134, 135, 136 (C), 143 (B), 148 (C)

E Morrall: 85, 86, 87

R Parker: 90 (T), 91, 102, 136 (B)

A. Potter: 14 (T), 23 (B), 24, 24 (Inset), 25 (Insets), 27, 38 (B)

Punch: 140 (T)

W R Reynolds: 14 (B), 23 (T), 40 (TR), 41 (T)

Mrs H C W Richardson: 9

A Sandbrook: 100

Soldier Magazine: 156, 159

Maj Gen J Spurling: 149 (B)

Lt Col Stanton: 34

R D Walls: 104 (C), 142 (TR), 146 (B), 147, 148 (T)